THE REAL SCIENCE BEHIND
T H E Ⓧ − F I L E S™

MICROBES, METEORITES, AND MUTANTS

Anne Simon, Ph.D.

Simon & Schuster Paperbacks
New York . London Toronto Sydney

SIMON & SCHUSTER PAPERBACKS
Rockefeller Center
1230 Avenue of the Americas
New York, NY 10020

For information about special discounts for bulk purchases,
please contact Simon & Schuster Special Sales:
1-800-456-6798 or business@simonandschuster.com.

Designed by Ruth Lee

Manufactured in the United States of America

10 9 8 7 6 5 4 3 2 1

The Library of Congress has cataloged the hardcover
edition as follows:

Simon, Anne Elizabeth, date.
The real science behind the X-files : microbes, meteorites,
and mutants / Anne Simon.
p.   cm.
1. Life sciences. 2. X-files (Television program).
3. Genetics. I. Title.
QH309.S554 1999
570—dc21   99-16531

ISBN-13:   978-0-684-85617-9
ISBN-10:   0-684-85617-4
ISBN-13:   978-0-7432-8495-0 (Pbk)
ISBN-13:   0-7432-8495-X (Pbk)

Text excerpted from previously published edition.
The full text, including chapters four through six,
is available at your local bookstore.

To MAYO SIMON,

for passing down the writing genes,

and SONDRA SIMON,

for being the world's greatest mom.

Contents

THE REAL SCIENCE BEHIND

THE (X)-FILES™

Foreword

MULDER

I have plenty of theories. What has me stumped is why Bureau
policy is to label these cases as unexplained phenomena and
ignore them.

           (to the point)

Do you believe in the existence of extraterrestrials?

SCULLY

I've never given it much thought.

MULDER

As a scientist.

SCULLY

Logically, I'd have to say no. Given the distances needed to
travel from the far reaches of space, the energy require-
ments would exceed—

MULDER

—Conventional wisdom. That girl in Oregon—she's the fourth
member of her graduating class to die under mysterious circumstances. When convention and science offer no answers,
might we not consider the fantastic as a plausibility?

"The X-Files Pilot Episode, 1992"

I'm often asked a question by strangers, by reporters, by TV executives, and by fans of *The X-Files:* Where do you get your ideas? It's an obvious question given the kind of show *The X-Files* is, but I never have a good comeback and usually try to make a joke. It seems counter to the creative process to give a straight answer. Where do they think the ideas come from? They come from our imaginations— mine and the other writers' on *The X-Files.* Likewise the characters of Mulder and Scully, who'd come to me bidden and unbidden in the summer of 1992 when I was creating the show. The process is mysterious, or as the scientific Scully would tell you, simply an unexplained phenomenon. The truth is out there.

Actually, the truth is, more often than not, the ideas which become *X-Files* stories are rooted in hard science, and even when they are not generated as such, they're built on a foundation of scientific convention. The point of view of the series is essentially Agent Scully's, the scientific counterpoint to Agent Mulder's belief in the supernatural. The rational versus the irrational. Her sober approach is the skeptical counterintuitive to Mulder's postmodern fanaticism. It's her science (she's a medical doctor) on which the science fiction depends. All the forces, creatures, acts, and apparitions that Mulder may throw at her—six years' worth at this writing—she believes science can explain. And if not now, eventually. Her faith in the empirical process is equal to Mulder's in the fantastic. (Even more so, if you consider the "I Want to Believe" poster that hangs on Agent Mulder's office wall; he is working through his convictions, while Agent Scully has her feet planted firmly on the alien-uninhabited ground.)

The problem is, Agent Scully is rarely, if ever, right. Her science is unequal to the wonders of the universe, or at least to the wonders of Mulder's multitude of FBI case files. Prove it, she's asked rhetorically each week, and each week she can't quite. It's not that she's wrong, but by necessity she is left without any good explanation. She and her methods are inadequate and can't ever seem to wipe the smile off Agent Mulder's face at the end of each episode.

And it is a problem, or so it's been pointed out to me, most demonstrably by the Committee for Scientific Investigation into Claims of the Paranormal (CSICOP) who invited me to speak to several hundred of its members (Nobel winners among them) in Buffalo, New York, several summers ago. They had me for lunch, as it were, where I looked around and saw few such smiles as Mulder's in the big university meeting hall. It felt as if I were standing before an army of Agent Scullys who were branding me a prime time purveyor of "pseudoscience." As if I alone were responsible for all the loopy, looney trends in angels and aliens, in superstition, and even in fundamentalism. I was threatening to destroy yet another generation of minds by feeding them more bogus claptrap. Carl Sagan, one of CSICOP's most prominent scientists, had just published *The Demon-Haunted World,* which took to task people just like me.

I was arguably guilty to some degree, the popularity of the show irrefutable evidence of this. Agent Mulder does believe in extraterrestrial life and in the government conspiracy to keep its existence a secret from the world. He does believe in vampires, ghosts, tulpas, revenants, PK, telekinesis, reincarnation, voodoo, astral projection, eidolons, zombies, werewolves, and sewer-dwelling human flukeworms from Chernobyl. (To be fair, what he really believes in is the "extreme possibility" of these things. If he believed in them absolutely, why bother investigating them?!) How could I defend myself, and why even try? To make matters worse, my formal science education ended somewhere around college graduation, and I hadn't been such a great student. I was going to meet the enemy, a large number of whom were college professors, and I was unarmed. From where did a television producer get such audacity? (Some would call that a tautology.)

To this question I did have a good answer, in the name of Anne Simon. Like my accusers, she is a college professor and a skeptic and, like Agent Scully, has a trust and faith in the scientific process. She is not just a teacher but a researcher. Her work with plant viruses has made her part of an international community of scientists pushing the limits of practical and theoretical understanding of plant genetics. I'd met Anne through her mother and father, who are friends of my wife, and near the end of the first season of *The X-Files* I'd learned with pleasant surprise she was a fan of the show. This was at the same time I was working to fully develop the show's "mythology," the alien conspiracy Agent Mulder believed in, so I'd given Anne a call. I told her I was uninterested in aliens per se, in the "literature" and its devotees, and also in the spaceships and looking to the skies (we'd seen so much of this, there hardly seemed anywhere new to go, particularly given TV budgets). I wanted to take a scientific approach to the subject, both psychological and genetic, and to build my extended story line on accepted theories and fact. (This was my intention from the start. I would tell the writers and directors ad nauseam that the show was only as scary as it seemed believable, and only as believable as it seemed real or plausible.) My idea for the first-season series finale was an experiment that involved genetic material Agent Mulder had stumbled on, which Agent Scully would learn was undeniably extraterrestrial QED. From Anne I got the building blocks of the mystery, literally: genes, chromosomes, proteins, nucleotides. I also got a careful script reader who would call me on inaccuracies in the science, and, through our long conversations, I even got from her the title of the episode: "The Erlenmeyer Flask." (The episode would go on to be nominated for an Edgar Award by the Mystery Writers of America.)

Why would Anne Simon throw in with a heretic like me? Because she'd come to science and to being a scientist through her love of science fiction. And this is what I told the CSICOP members over lunch. Anne has been and continues to be a voracious reader of science fiction novels, both the futuristic and the more speculative works closer to the stories that we tell on *The X-Files*. She, like many scientists I've met, has great enthusiasm for her work, and approaches it with imagination and appreciation for ideas. Which is what *X-Files* writers do, actually. Creative speculation seems to be the force that drives science forward, rather than the limiting conventions of accepted truth. I'm reminded of Dr. Tom Kaufman, a scientist Anne suggested I contact at Indiana University, with whom I spent a wonderful day learning about his genetic experiments on the *Drosophila* fly. His work became the basis for a Frankenstein story I wrote called, "The Postmodern Prometheus," about an amateur scientist who creates a son by manipulating human genes like Dr. Kaufman does his flies'. This is something we may very well see applied in our lifetimes. (I also told the committee about another professor with a love of science fiction. Someone much closer to me, my younger brother Craig Carter, who teaches material science at MIT.)

If Anne Simon was affected by her early exposure to ideas, might not *The X-Files* inspire future scientists? I believe it will, and could very well continue to for years to come. It's fair to say no other long-running dramatic television show has used such a wide (and strange!) variety of science fact in its storytelling: medicine, genetics, cryonics, cosmology, quantum physics, dendrochronology, to name but a few disciplines. And this in a medium criticized for pandering to the masses. And might the science fiction of *The X-Files* even be regarded someday as science convention? Both a sheep named Dolly and a rock from Mars have made news during the show's run. (Meeting Stephen Hawking some years after my CSICOP lunch, I asked him his feelings about science fiction or pseudoscience. His reply was that science and science fiction had something to give each other, and that "science fiction is no more pseudo than cosmology.")

What I believe Anne Simon ultimately appreciates, and what I asserted to my hosts that afternoon in Buffalo, is that stories and storytelling are essential to life. As Nietzsche and Ibsen knew, life requires life-supporting myths and metaphors. Or even illusions. Freud said myths are public dreams and dreams private myths, both essential to the psyche. Or the soul. Science demystifies the world. It's meant to reassure us, as Georges Braque set forth, whereas the purpose of art is to disturb. The relationship between the two is also essential and should be fostered and celebrated rather than rooted out. Or, as I told the CSICOP folks, science tells you your cell phone might give you a brain tumor, whereas art allows it might be how your long dead Uncle Harry reaches you from the Great Beyond. For which I got a polite round of applause, and after signing a few autographs, was bid adieu. I've never heard from them since.

—Chris Carter, creator of
The X-Files, March 1999

Introduction

In September 1993 I read a description in *TV Guide* for a new show called *The X-Files*. As a fan of science fiction, I found the synopsis to be intriguing—the adventures of two FBI agents who investigate cases of a paranormal nature. My expectations were not particularly high given the channel the show was on. The still fledgling Fox network was better known for urban situation comedies and bubblegum-chewing narcs than serious science fiction.

Was I surprised. The first few minutes of the show were mesmerizing: spooky music, brooding actors, and realistic dialogue added up to an intelligence and quality unusual for any network. When the opening credits rolled and I saw the name of the show's creator, Chris Carter, I thought, could this possibly be the Chris Carter whom I knew? The writer-surfer who married my mother's good friend, scriptwriter Dori Pierson? Last I had heard, Chris and Dori were working for Disney's Buena Vista Studios. Still, knowing how often my scriptwriter father moved from one job to the next meant that anything was possible.

By the end of the first episode, I was hooked. Not only was *The X-Files* great science fiction, but as a bonus, the lead character was a woman doctor with a "background in the hard sciences." A scientist as a main character in a serious television show. And one who was not a nerdy, bow-tied, absentminded, congenial fool or a sinister madman developing a formula to destroy the world. The refreshing Dana Scully was actually being portrayed as a realistic scientist. Attractive (I did say this was realistic), intelligent, and dedicated to her work, Scully was a character I, a woman scientist, could relate to.

Without the efforts of my eighth-grade biology teacher, I might never have become a scientist. Mrs. Webb had inexplicably placed me in a ninth-grade science class as my first elective course at Paul Revere Junior High School. This gesture, poorly appreciated at the time, led to classes at the Los Angeles Museum of Natural History followed by enrollment at the University of California at San Diego. My interests turned from marine biology, the initial major of many from the Pacific Palisades fun-in-the-sun crowd, to genetics after I took some stimulating college courses. In my senior year, one of my professors suggested Indiana University for graduate school. Four years later, I received a Ph.D. in genetics for solving the mystery of why some animal cells have mutation rates far beyond the norm. By the way, aliens were not involved.

After finishing graduate school, I needed to remain at Indiana University while I waited for my husband to get his Ph.D. In order to stay at the same university, I was advised—strongly—to switch fields; otherwise I put future academic positions at risk. (To clarify the logic of this advice to nonacademicians, switching fields shows the proper adventurous spirit thought necessary for a budding scientist, which counters the more timid impression of not wanting to transfer away from one's training environment.) As a result, I decided to study how plant embryos develop. Not thoroughly enamored of the subject and eager to revisit the Pacific Ocean, I headed back to San Diego and began studying viruses (by this time, relatives were wondering if I was ever going to get a "real" job). Viruses and I agreed with each other, and I continued in the field of virology after getting that real job as an assistant professor at the University of Massachusetts at Amherst.

Five years after settling down to a life of research and teaching, and midway through *The X-Files'* first season, I received a phone call from my mother. Did I know that Dori's husband, Chris Carter, had a new series called *The X-Files*? (So it *was* Chris's show.) Chris, knowing that I was a scientist, had asked my mother if I would mind discussing some science questions for one of his scripts. She told me that she had given him my phone number. Moms do know best.

Chris called the following day. He was delighted to hear that I was a fan of the show, particularly since the ratings were not quite what they are today. Chris described his idea for an episode in which a scientist suffering from cancer finds some alien tissue that might be a cure. The scientist is planning to test the tissue for harmful effects on children at a large state-run institution (paralleling a news story several years ago about scientific experiments performed on institutionalized children without their consent). I told Chris that a scientist dying of cancer would probably subject himself to the experiment given the long history of scientists experimenting on themselves. Chris liked that idea and went on to ask: If someone handed a microbiologist an unclassified microbe, how would it be studied? I described three steps: grow more of the organism by culturing it in an Erlenmeyer flask; visualize it under a microscope; and examine its genetic material, its DNA. After going into depth on all three of these procedures, Chris needed an answer to his most important question: What experimental result would instantly suggest an extraterrestrial origin for the organism? Chris was waiting, so I quickly thought up a little science with a science fiction twist—some results that would make me reach for the phone if I ever encountered such a strange microbe.[1]

A few weeks after our conversation, the finished script for "The Erlenmeyer Flask" arrived by express mail. Since I was used to reading my father's science fiction scripts (*Marooned, Phase IV, Futureworld, Man from Atlantis*), I could vividly picture the fantastic episode that would emerge on the screen. There were, however, a few scientific inaccuracies in the description of one scientist's area of expertise—the human genome project—and in the conversation between Scully and scientist Anne Carpenter. But these problems were easily corrected, mostly with the change of a single word or phrase. When I watched "The Erlenmeyer Flask" on TV, I followed along with my copy of the script. To my delight, Chris had used every suggestion. Soon afterward, he sent me one of the first *X-Files* T-shirts emblazoned with the phrase "The Truth Is Out There." I remember thinking that he was crazy to have T-shirts made up with the logo from a TV show and expect people to buy them. In retrospect, this thought

[1]Explained in detail in Chapter 2.

was ample evidence that an aptitude for science doesn't necessarily translate into a head for business.

As *X-Files* episodes continued to air, the central nature of science and Scully's role in the series became evident. Scully provides realistic scientific interpretations behind the decidedly odd events. Scully is the quintessential scientist. She gathers information and bases her hypotheses on that evidence. She also keeps partner Fox Mulder from rushing to unsupported conclusions. Mulder, searching for the answers behind his sister's childhood abduction, readily formulates the most outlandish explanations for what are, granted, rather unusual happenings. If Mulder finds that a person has been buried in mud in a standing position and a corpse is removed from a coffin, then it must be the trees in an orchard that are killing people and raiding graves, guided by the psychic emanations from a deranged woman possessed by the spirit of her abusive father. Scully, adhering to the scientifically sound precept that the simplest explanation is likely to be correct, tries to convince Mulder that the dead root system of the diseased trees combined with substantial rainfall created the muddy sinkholes that swallowed up the townspeople.

And therein lies the controversy. Controversy that reaches all the way to the editorial pages of one of the world's most eminent scientific periodicals, the British journal *Nature*. For as *X-Files* fans know, Scully is usually wrong. The trees *are* being guided by the brain waves of a psychotic woman. The concept that science cannot explain all "unnatural" occurrences and the believable nature of the show's science fiction scenarios leave *The X-Files* open to critics who claim that it is "antiscience." What the critics of the show have lost sight of is that *The X-Files* is science fiction. If Scully's mundane explanations were correct more often, it is doubtful that the series would have lasted into its second season, let alone achieve its current cult status.

Those who see *The X-Files* as promoting pseudoscience (and therefore antiscience) are missing the point. Viewers, especially high school and college students, who make up the core of the fan base, are seeing scientists portrayed in a favorable light, perhaps for the first time. Few outside of the scientific world are personally acquainted with a scientist and therefore have only inaccurate fictional characterizations (usually unfavorable) with which to base their feelings. The portrayal of scientists in most television and feature films as remote, emotionless, obsessed individuals does little to attract bright young minds to the fascinating world of science.

Granted, the scientists in *The X-Files* don't have all the answers and their results are frequently open to many possible interpretations. But this is precisely what is faced by research scientists on a daily basis. The goal of scientists is to solve mysteries: How do viruses reproduce? Why does a particular virus infect some organisms and not others? Why are some viruses deadly while others go unnoticed? These are just some of the puzzles that I face daily in my own research. And just like the adventures of Mulder and Scully, answers lead to more puzzles, dead ends loom around every corner, and a mind open to remote possibilities is the key ingredient behind finding the truth.

The characters on *The X-Files*—some of them, anyway—are pretty accurate portraits of contemporary working scientists. Dana Scully doesn't claim a knowledge of botany through nuclear physics (like a certain stranded castaway). Rather, she uses her medical degree to perform autopsies and her knowledge of genetics and biochemistry to conduct experiments. As with any scientist, when the investigation leads to areas outside her expertise, she consults with other experts. In a refreshing departure from the norm, scientists on *The X-Files* are more likely to be aiding the investigations than perpetrating the crimes. While many bizarre and completely fictional creatures populate *X-Files* episodes, the scientific investigations of these creatures are based on reality. The proper experiments are conducted; the correct microscopes are used; evidence is gathered and conclusions are based on that evidence. To achieve such accuracy on the show requires an attention to detail and extra effort from the writers that fans can see and appreciate— and many of these fans are scientists.

I am often asked why I care so much about scientific accuracy on a science fiction show. The answer is simple. As a scientist, it usually isn't possible to watch science in movies or TV without wincing. The microscopes are wrong; the language is wrong; cures of viral infections are instantaneous; organisms are described as being part bacteria, part virus (analogous to saying part watermelon, part speck of dust). What I find frustrating is that many problems could have been fixed without affecting the plot—if only the writers had spent a few minutes consulting with a working scientist.

My association with *The X-Files* has involved a number of scripts (all written by Chris Carter, a true creative genius), including the *X-Files* movie, *Fight the Future*. I feel fortunate to have played a small role in helping to ground *The X-Files* in real science. However, the average viewer of a television show that prides itself on its depiction of realistic and very scary creatures can have difficulty deciphering the line between science and science fiction. The goal of this book is to explain to nonscientists the real science behind *The X-Files*. To use the show as a springboard to examine the many science issues that are blended into plots—hot topics like cloning, aging, genetic engineering, and life on other planets. In an age where science is transforming the food we eat, the information that we process, and the health care we receive, knowledge of basic scientific tenets can no longer be thought of as too complicated, too boring, or confined to the realm of stereotypic white-coated geeks. Besides the mere facts, I also hope to convey the excitement of biological science, which abounds with creatures and mysteries every bit as strange as any appearing on *The X-Files*.

Enjoy the journey.

1

Hidden and Hungry

Introduction

```
MIDDLESEX COUNTY PSYCH HOSPITAL—DAY
ANGLE ON CORNER OF CELL
```

Where, squeezed back behind a series of pipes running vertically up the wall, A GRAYISH HUMAN FORM remains perfectly still. Its skin is mottled and scarred and it appears to be smooth and hairless, coated with a shiny layer of clear slime, like a snail or a slug. Because its face is obscured by the pipes, the only way you can tell it is alive is by an unnatural pulsing in its neck, similar to a bullfrog in this respect.

```
INT. CORRIDOR—CONTINUOUS
RESUME MULDER, SCULLY IN CORRIDOR
```

MULDER
I don't know if you can see, but it has no sex organs. It's genderless.

SCULLY
Platyhelminthes are often hermaphroditic. This is amazing, Mulder. Its vestigial features look parasitic, but it seems to have primate physiology.

(beat)
Where the hell did it come from?

MULDER
(with due irony)
I don't know. But it looks like I'm going to have to tell Skin-
ner that the suspect is a blood sucking worm after all.

—"The Host"

The largest life form on Earth is the six-thousand-ton intercon-
nected quaking aspen in Utah. The smallest is bacteria, about eight
hundred thousandths of an inch across. With living creatures available in virtually every size in between, life is present in seemingly infinite varieties. Unless you're surrounded by a barren desert, walk
outside and look around at the hundreds of plants, insects, birds,
mammals, and fungi in your vicinity. Peer into a drop of pond water
and you'll find a world of microorganisms that when magnified look
every bit as uncanny as the *X-Files'* legendary flukeman. Any spoon-
ful of dirt contains thousands of different bacteria, many of which
have never been identified. At this very moment, in the cubic yard of
air at the tip of your nose, hundreds of thousands of microscopic bacteria, viruses, fungal spores, algae, and pollen grains are floating by.
Over 50 million species share this planet with us, the products of
nearly 4 billion years of evolution.

I probably wouldn't get an argument from even the most devoted *X-Files* fans if I pointed out that flukemen weren't likely to ever
peek out of your toilet. What comes closer to the line between science and science fiction, and is therefore much more disquieting, are
the *X-Files* creatures that don't require a supernatural origin. These
are the organisms hidden in places not normally seen by humans—in
volcanic rocks, within ancient trees, frozen beneath the arctic ice, or
deep in the heart of unexplored rain forests. Maybe it's simple,
everyday fungi, floating invisibly in the air, which emerge from obscurity to become deadly disease agents. When you consider that
only a few percent of the organisms on planet Earth have been identified, the chance of finding new and not always friendly creatures is
not only within the realm of possibility, it is a virtual certainty.

Each day, previously unknown creatures are being discovered, and not just in exotic locations far from civilization. In my own bailiwick of Massachusetts, naturalists have been examining fields, forests, lakes, and rivers for almost three hundred years—plenty of time to turn over every rock, dig through every swamp, and traverse every forest. But all it takes is a dip in the Connecticut River—the first river in the United States to be navigated by European settlers—to realize the fallacy of such a statement. The Connecticut River is a beautiful, pastoral body of water that slowly meanders four hundred miles from the Canadian border through the fertile valleys of Western Massachusetts before finishing its journey at the Long Island Sound. Recent underwater explorations by my University of Massachusetts colleague Dr. Edward Klekowski revealed the remains of a previously unknown Ice Age lake hidden below the rippling surface. The proglacial Lake Hitchcock left an imprint of clay sediments in the Connecticut River that are now covered with enormous numbers of larvae of a fly not known before to exist. Other strange creatures inhabit deeper regions of the river. A crack in the Earth some 200 million years ago caused the base of the river to drop 130 feet below the surface in some locations. In the inky depths lies a world only recently explored—a world of giant sponges and mosslike animals that form colonies eerily resembling plants. While these creatures may not spark the imagination like Scotland's Loch Ness Monster or the *X-Files'* own Big Blue Serpent of Heuvelmans Lake, they are real-life equivalents—organisms imagined but never before seen.

Twenty years ago, scientists would have limited the regions where life abounds to the surface of the land and ocean depths where light is not completely absent. After all, living creatures need energy and the primary source of energy is the sun. Scientists figured out long ago that green plants and some microorganisms use the sun's energy directly in the process called photosynthesis—the combining of carbon dioxide and water to form sugars. These sugars then serve as a secondary source of energy for the plants and a primary source of energy for the rest of us. Only on land and in the ocean were oxygen and minerals thought to be sufficiently abundant to form the molecules imperative for life. Underground worlds filled with real-life equivalents of Jules Verne's Cretaceous creatures seemed biologically impossible.

These notions disappeared in 1979 when an astonishing article appeared in the journal *Science*. The most remote region thought to exist at the time, the bottom of deep ocean trenches, had been considered by scientists to be a graveyard of dying crabs and rotting fish. Instead, a world was found teeming with life that did not rely on the sun. Researchers were amazed to discover acres of mollusks and tube worms, some over ten feet long, feeding on bacteria that also don't need the sun. Rather, the bacteria derive energy from the blistering furnace of the Earth's interior. Liquid methane and gaseous hydrogen sulfide that slowly seep through hydrothermal vents contain enough chemical energy for deep-dwelling bacteria to generate other types of cellular energy. Bacteria that live near these holes in the ocean's crust must survive in sizzling temperatures once thought to be unendurable for living creatures. Temperatures reach 235°F near ocean vents, and only the extreme pressure of the depths keeps nearby seawater from boiling. What was once considered the most inhospitable of habitats is now believed to be a warm and homey domicile for wet denizens of the very deep.

Finding organisms that are able to use energy sources other than the sun opened up another intriguing possibility. If life doesn't require the sun, couldn't there be life below our feet? Not the dinosaurs of Verne's lost world, but maybe tiny creatures able to live within the near-solid rock. One of the most astonishing scientific discoveries of the past ten years was finding that the abundance and variety of organisms living on the surface of the Earth and in the water was only the tip of life's iceberg. Hidden beneath our feet, below the ocean floor and the arctic ice caps, in temperatures reaching 235°F and in rocks so dense that water can take centuries to permeate, live communities of microorganisms. And not just a few isolated species. Tens of thousands of different strains of bacteria have already been identified that live as much as 2.5 miles below the continental crust, the very limits that sweltering temperatures permit life. Any lower down and the sizzling heat would cause a cell's biomolecules to be destroyed faster than they can function.

Dr. Thomas Gold of Cornell University has calculated that pound for pound, there may be as much life living below the ground as there is life on the planet's surface. Creatures that live in this hidden underground world have been separated from surface dwellers for hundreds of millions of years. There is no oxygen in most places, so organisms must find a way to survive in its absence. There is little water or food, so creatures must learn to live while thirsty and starving. These seemingly miserable microorganisms are encased in tiny crevasses in rock and need hundreds, maybe even thousands of years to reproduce by dividing their tiny selves in two.

But if you're simply looking for some new species, it isn't necessary to drill miles underground or plunge into deep water. The earth is occupied by an amazing variety of creatures whose universe is the body of another organism. Endosymbiont is what biologists call creatures that live in harmony with their host in a mutually beneficial arrangement. Endopathogens exploit the host for their own gain; by the time an endopathogen is finished with its host, the host is usually dead.

As humans, we like to think that we are the masters of our bodies. But sharing our innards are billions of bacteria, protozoa, viruses, and fungi. These invisible microbes are everywhere—in our mouth, ears, nose, stomach, and skin. Just days after a baby is born, the microbes start pouring in. Cough, and 10 million microbes shoot out into the air. Scrubbing the scalp to remove the millions of bacteria residing in each square inch is only a temporary fix since other little microbes soon move in. There are, by the way, more bacteria in your gut alone than there are human cells in your entire body.

If your perceptions of the world are similar to Fox Mulder's, you might wonder if the microbes inhabiting your body are engaged in a sinister conspiracy instigated by evil forces in the government to take over your carcass. Dana Scully, however, would explain that you wouldn't be alive and healthy without your little guests. Most colonizing microbes are endosymbionts—you scratch their tiny backs and they scratch yours. Microbes in your intestines make several vitamins for your well-being. *Escherichia coli* bacteria are like little factories making and exporting vitamin K and some B vitamins. If you aren't getting enough protein in your diet, *Klebsiella* bacteria can provide your cells with some raw chemical materials needed to help you make proteins. Some of the hundred thousand bacteria per square inch of your skin help protect you from less benevolent microbes. One of your surface bacteria, *Propionibacterium,* produces an acid that helps keep harmful bacteria away, such as the typhoid bacteria, *Salmonella typhi.*

But while some microbes are friendly, others are decidedly not. Infectious diseases have been a thorn in the side of man since civilization began. Concentrate enough people in one location and creatures that cause disease, known as pathogens, can spread from one person to another. When trade routes to nearby towns were established, pathogens tagged along with the caravans. Intrepid explorers seeking adventure beyond the ocean's horizon brought little stowaways to new continents—rats, fleas, lice, bacteria, and viruses. The history of man is a history of infectious diseases. Epidemics of plague, smallpox, typhus, cholera, measles, and a host of plant pathogens wiped out armies, caused widespread famine, and decimated cities. The bubonic plague or "black death" in the fourteenth century indiscriminately killed 25 million Europeans. The influenza pandemic in 1918 killed a half percent of the world's population, some 20 million to 25 million people, including 600,000 Americans, most in the prime of their life. It wasn't the ingenuity of FBI agents that finally conquered the plague bacterium in the Middle Ages or the virus responsible for the lethal influenza. People susceptible to the bacteria or virus died. People who were naturally resistant lived. The pathogens died out when they ran out of people to infect.

While pathogens in *The X-Files* tend to come from exotic locations—beneath the arctic ice or within tropical rain forests—many new diseases in the past twenty-five years have emerged from locations much closer to home. In 1976, 182 people attending the American Legion convention in Philadelphia brought back home with them a deadly souvenir from the Bellevue-Stratford Hotel—a tiny bacterium that had not previously made its presence known. Thirty-four men died of what is now called Legionnaire's disease. The following year, the Centers for Disease Control (CDC) isolated the bacteria responsible for the disease and named it *Legionella*. Since then, dozens of outbreaks of *Legionella* have been reported from San Francisco to Connecticut, with hundreds of other outbreaks around the world.

As anyone with access to a newspaper knows, *E. coli* serotype O157:H7 has become a notorious food contaminant. This strain of *E. coli* was unheard of before 1982. Since then, there have been sixty major outbreaks in the United States. The most severe occurrence was in 1993, when more than seven hundred people in four states became infected by eating undercooked hamburger at a fast food restaurant. Each year in the United States alone, eating food contaminated with dangerous bacteria sickens 6 million to 80 million people, causes 9,000 deaths, and costs an estimated 5 billion dollars. Eating beef isn't the only way to come in contact with this lethal new bacterium. *E. coli* has been found in such unlikely foods as unpasteurized apple juice, salad vegetables, yogurt, and drinking water.

New disease agents are also lurking in forests, lakes, and reservoirs. Lyme disease, caused by bacteria-infected ticks, was not a problem before 1982. Today, it's a common concern when walking in forested areas in the Northeast. Lyme disease emerged from its hiding place within forests when more people decided to live in houses surrounded by trees. *Cryptosporidium,* a protozoan parasite that contaminates drinking water and infects the digestive tract, emerged in 1976. In 1993, the drinking water in Milwaukee, Wisconsin, became contaminated with *Cryptosporidium,* causing more than 400,000 people to become sick and 100 to die. As many as 7 percent of all diarrhea cases in the United States are now attributed to this parasite.

With modern medicine and improvements in technology, why are the numbers of deaths due to infectious diseases climbing higher every year? People are living longer and healthier lives, yet more people will die of tuberculosis this year than in any year in history. Mulder would probably attribute the large numbers of disease outbreaks to the increasing number of reported UFO sightings since the 1940s. However, to find the real reasons for the increase in infectious diseases, one need look no further than, well, modern medicine and improvements in technology.

So why is modern medicine making us sick? Medical technology, like organ transplantation and cancer therapy, means a longer life for people with chronic diseases but also more people with compromised immune systems. This growing segment of the population is most vulnerable to diseases. People with weakened immune systems become reservoirs for high levels of disease agents that can be transmitted to other people. As more people have weakened immune systems, microbes that were once thought of as harmless are now viewed as significant problems. *Cryptosporidium,* for example, is a previously innocuous parasite that now causes between 10 and 20 percent of the intestinal infections in AIDS patients. More ominously, *Cryptosporidium* is now able to infect healthy hosts.

Modern medicine also prolongs the life of people in general. The number of people over the age of seventy-four is 400 percent higher in 1995 than it was in 1950. People who are older are at greater risk for a variety of illnesses. One possible reason why older people are more susceptible to invasion by pathogens is that their stomachs are no longer as acidic, reducing the efficacy of a major body defense against disease agents that are eaten.

Healthier eating habits are also paradoxically contributing to new outbreaks of disease. Those nutritious raw vegetables and fruits can be contaminated with microorganisms while they are being grown, harvested, or delivered to neighborhood supermarkets or restaurants. Cooking vegetables does more than cause vitamins to leach out; it kills many contaminating organisms hidden on the surface or inside foods. Between 1990 and 1997, disease outbreaks have been associated with such healthy pastimes as eating sliced cantaloupe, green onions, unpasteurized cider, freshly squeezed orange juice, lettuce, raspberries, alfalfa sprouts, sliced tomatoes, and frozen strawberries. Our modern lifestyles also include many more visits to restaurants, where 80 percent of reported food-related outbreaks take place.

Modern technology is also a major contributor to increases in harmful microorganisms. Modern food technology means an increasing number of centralized processing facilities. Instead of family dairies providing milk to the local population, huge milk factories now supply entire regions. Contaminated milk from a large Midwestern dairy caused 250,000 people to become ill from *Salmonella* bacteria. Hen houses don't contain five hundred birds anymore, they contain hundreds of thousands of birds, and an undetected contamination of eggs can cause infections to break out over multistate areas. Technological advances in keeping huge buildings cool are also conduits for disease. There were no problems with *Legionella* before massive air-conditioning and plumbing systems gave the bacteria a friendly breeding environment. Powerful vents that sweep over vats of water containing *Legionella* spread microdroplets of bacteria into the air within buildings. Breathe in the droplets and *Legionella* comes in as well. Even such innocuous advancements as vegetable misters in supermarkets can be a way of spreading *Legionella*.

With new infectious agents being discovered on a yearly basis, the search for new treatments must remain a high priority. Fortunately, humans aren't the only ones who need to protect themselves against invasion by bacteria. Evolution has led to many organisms making small substances—antibiotics—that kill invading bacteria. The antibiotic penicillin, considered by many to be the miracle drug of the twentieth century, was discovered in a fungus by Alexander Fleming in 1928. Penicillin works by keeping bacteria from building bigger walls around their cells while the cells continue to grow. Without an expanding cell wall, the bacteria literally blow themselves up. Penicillin has no harmful effect on human cells because our cells don't build such walls. The manufacture and distribution of penicillin during World War II was followed by streptomycin in 1944, which was highly effective against tuberculosis. Streptomycin and many other antibiotics block bacterial machines called ribosomes from making proteins. Human cells also have ribosomes, but they are different enough from those of bacteria to be unaffected by this class of antibiotic.

Of the thousands of compounds so far identified that kill bacteria, only fifty don't also harm human cells. Still, with such an arsenal of antibiotics, U.S. Surgeon General William Stewart in 1969 gave congressional testimony that we could soon "close the book on infectious disease." Too bad no one thought to inform the bacteria. Anyone who doubts Charles Darwin's theory of survival of the fittest has only to look at the simple bacterium. Antibiotics work because they interfere with the functioning of important bacterial proteins. To interfere with the workings of a protein, the antibiotic must attach to the protein, like the fitting together of two jigsaw puzzle pieces. If the side of the bacterial protein that connects with the antibiotic becomes altered, the pieces no longer fit together. When this happens, the bacterium is able to ignore the presence of the antibiotic and grow without constraint.

Any time antibiotics are used, there is a risk that one of the millions of bacteria being treated is a mutant and makes proteins that don't attach to the antibiotic.[1] While this mutant bacterium may not seem as dangerous as the various *X-Files* mutants, its potential for

[1] Exactly how mutations affect DNA and proteins will be covered in Chapter 3.

harm is much greater. This bacterium will survive the antibiotic treatment that kills all the nonmutant bacteria. A few days later, the mutant bacterium will have multiplied into billions of bacteria that also ignore the antibiotic. As the mutant bacteria spread from one person to another, deadly infections can result unless other antibiotics exist to kill the bacteria. Ironically, hospitals have become breeding grounds for mutant bacteria due to the presence of so many patients with weakened immune systems and by the widespread use of antibiotics.

There is a risk that antibiotic-resistant bacteria can be generated every time antibiotics are prescribed. Every year in the United States, more than 4 million antibiotic prescriptions are given to people who have common colds or the flu, infections caused by viruses. Antibiotics have absolutely no effect on viruses. In a recent Canadian study, 40 percent of physicians gave antibiotics to patients who demanded them knowing full well that they would have no effect whatsoever. Due to such indiscriminate use of antibiotics, the best weapons against bacterial infections may soon be blunted. For this reason, pharmaceutical companies have stepped up the hunt for new antibacterial compounds by searching for more organisms that have found different ways of killing bacteria.

And where will they find such organisms? In places where creatures are still hiding—deep within tropical rain forests or frozen in amber or in rocks underground.

With so much life waiting to be discovered, whether miles beneath the ground, in the heart of unexplored rain forests, hidden inside other organisms, or in the river down the road, it's no wonder that the perils of what lies hidden is a major theme in science fiction. In *The X-Files*, strange, alien worms lurk below the surface of Alaskan ice and feed off the anger of the hosts they inhabit; extinct mites emerge from old-growth trees ready to try a new delicacy—dried-up loggers; fungal spores that inhabit volcanic rocks find human bodies much more to their liking; bugs in the rain forests have a big surprise in store for those who are looking for the next miracle health product; and let's not forget El Chupacabra, the Mexican goatsucker. The fictional organisms that populate these episodes are alive only within the minds of the scriptwriters, yet the type of havoc that they wreak is not confined to the comfort of your television screen. While Mulder believes aliens lurk behind most unusual incidents, it is the plausible, scientific explanations given by Scully—based on the large number of real emerging pathogens—that make these creatures appear very, very real.

Worms on Ice

INT. MAIN BUILDING [ARCTIC COMPOUND]—NIGHT

SCULLY

A parasite shouldn't want to kill its host.

HODGE

No. No. This won't kill you, unless you try to extract it. Then it releases a poison, the black fluid that killed the pilot.

MULDER

You're saying it's possible this worm makes you want to kill others... That could explain what happened to the first team.

DASILVA

Or what could happen to us.

—"Ice"

In the *X-Files* episode "Ice," a cold but dedicated group of scientists and their faithful dog are innocently conducting global climate research in northern Alaska. Frozen in time, deep below the icy surface, is a record of the environmental conditions on Earth dating back as far as a few hundred thousand years. As the scientists study their latest batch of ice core samples, it's quite obvious (obvious, that is, to anyone with six years of postgraduate geophysical training) that 200,000 years ago, Java Man was enjoying his morning brew as dawn rose on another balmy day. Unfortunately, the scientists are consumed with generating ancient weather reports and forget to see the movie *The Thing* (either version). They don't realize that ice core samples should never be taken in the vicinity of buried meteors. Soon the only survivor in the remote outpost is their aggressive bor-

der collie. The only clue to their untimely demise: the cryptic message "We are not who we are."

FBI agents Fox Mulder and Dana Scully along with a crack team
of doctors and scientists race to the remote Alaskan base to investigate. Instead of finding the morphing alien monster from *The Thing*,
they discover that the demented dog has bizarre cells in its blood,
nodules reminiscent of bubonic plague, and a worm crawling around
below the skin at the base of its skull. Scully speculates that the unusual cells are the free-living juvenile stage, or larvae, that will eventually develop into the adult worm creature. The worm, in true
X-Files fashion, is unlike any previously identified worm but has features similar to a tapeworm—a scolex (weird head), suckers, and
hooks. The dog blood also contains a high level of ammonium hy-
droxide, matching the high level of ammonia in the ice core sample.
Mulder naturally makes the connection between the proximity of
the buried meteor and the original location of the ice core sample.
Undoubtedly shaken by the discovery of so many dead geophysicists,
Mulder is a little off (about 250 million years) on his speculation
about the age of the ice core sample. Nonetheless, he suggests that
the worm survived being rudely separated from the rest of its planet,
a long meteor cruise, and an extensive sojourn under the Alaskan
ice, because it originated on a planet with a frozen, ammonium-
soaked atmosphere.[2]

Why an alien worm would want to take up residence under the
skin of dogs and people becomes a matter of intense speculation between Scully and her fellow scientists. They determine that the wrig-
gly parasite attaches itself to the hypothalamus, a region at the base
of the brain. Removing the worm has a nasty side effect: death. However, having an alien parasitic worm attached to the hypothalamus
has its own severe consequences. While the hypothalamus comprises
only 1 percent of the human brain, it controls most of the basic and
primal behaviors. Without a functioning hypothalamus, eating,
drinking, sleeping, and sex would all be simply memories.

Before the worm can approach the tasty hypothalamus, it needs
to swim through the blood into the brain. The vast majority of the
brain is protected from foreign substances by a roadblock called the

---

[2]Speculations on life in such an atmosphere will be presented in Chapter 2.

blood-brain barrier. Without this barrier, few brain cells would remain for life's golden years. Brain cells come in limited numbers and are not replaced if carelessly destroyed by minute traces of toxic substances in the blood. The blood-brain barrier filters out most of the impurities in the blood before the blood enters the brain. Fortunately for the worm, the hypothalamus is one area of the brain that can be accessed by an alien worm. The hypothalamus has several regions that are not protected by the blood-brain barrier, since the cells of the hypothalamus must be able to sense the state of the body by checking out everything that's in the bloodstream. Feelings of dying of thirst on a hot summer day come from the hypothalamus sensing a high concentration of salt in the blood. Real parasitic worms can also directly infect human brains, probably by eating right through the barrier. The alien worm could therefore bypass the blood-brain barrier just in time for breakfast.

Scully is correct when she states that the hypothalamus is a "gland that secretes hormones." About ten major glands produce hormones in higher animals like humans. A hormone is a substance that is produced in one part of an organism and then travels to another part of the organism where it can cause certain cells to perform some function. In humans, hormones are one of the brain's methods of communicating messages to the rest of the body. Cells that are supposed to respond to the hormone have proteins called receptors either on the surface of the cell or inside the cell. The hormone and its receptor are like interlocking pieces of a jigsaw puzzle. If the mobile hormone puzzle piece floating around in the bloodstream comes in contact with a receptor puzzle piece on the surface of a cell and finds a precise fit, a series of events occurs inside the cell that usually results in the cell doing something new like producing a new protein. The job of the hypothalamus is to secrete tiny amounts of hormones that travel to the pituitary, a blueberry-sized gland just below the hypothalamus. The pituitary is a major hormone producer, regulating everything from milk production to adult height.

A good example of hormone action is the hormone insulin. Insulin is a small protein hormone made in the pancreas, a gland located just below the stomach. Indulging in a sugar-laden ice cream sundae with mountains of hot fudge, whipped cream, and a candied cherry leads to high levels of sugar in the bloodstream. The pancreas senses the sugar levels and causes insulin to be produced and released into the bloodstream. Once mobile, insulin attaches to any cell that contains the insulin receptor on its surface. When insulin and its receptor meet and fit together on the surface of a cell, doorways into the cell swing open, allowing all that delicious sugar floating around in the blood to enter. Once inside the cell, the sugar is converted into carbon dioxide, water, and the fuel of the cell, ATP.

People with diabetes mellitus are unable to make insulin so cells are never instructed to open up and let the glucose in. Sugar remains in the bloodstream, causing water to move out of cells to dilute out the sugar. High levels of water in the bloodstream cause the kidneys to increase urine output to remove the excess water along with all the sugar that should have been used for energy. If a cell doesn't get enough sugar, the body switches to using fats and protein for energy, which damages critical tissues and organs. Before 1920, diabetes meant a substantially shortened life span. Now diabetics can perform the function of their pancreas, monitoring levels of sugar in the bloodstream and taking insulin when necessary.

Scully and the other scientists correctly speculate that the unusual aggressive behavior of the ice station's men and dog could be due to the worm sucking on the hypothalamus. That's because the hypothalamus does more than just sense body conditions; it's also involved in controlling aggression. Electric shocks in the regions of the hypothalamus that control aggression can provoke aggressive responses in people, much like those experienced by the outpost scientists before they apparently killed each other. Cancer patients unfortunate enough to have tumors on their hypothalamus can also become very aggressive.

If the Alaskan worm has a preference for a particular region of the hypothalamus, it could invoke a particular type of aggression. Aggression is generally thought of as either offensive or defensive. Offensive aggression is fighting for social status. Defensive aggression is protecting children. The aggressive behavior of the dog and the scientist who become infected are more offensive in nature, in line with the worm attaching to the hypothalamus in the upper middle portion, close to the front of the brain. Harboring an alien worm with an appetite for brain could certainly cause the afflicted individuals to feel that they "are not who they are."

Scully and the other scientists speculate that the worms suck on the hypothalamus to make the host aggressive so that the chemical acetylcholine can flood the brain. Acetylcholine would then be eaten by the worms, which probably have worked up quite an appetite after fasting for a few hundred million years. Acetylcholine is a small chemical called a neurotransmitter, which helps nerve cells carry electric signals. When skeletal muscles are stimulated to move an arm or a leg, it's a matter of nerve cells communicating to the muscle cells. The chemical messenger in this tête-à-tête is acetylcholine. For each muscle cell that is stimulated by a nerve cell, about 10 million molecules of acetylcholine are required.

Just as presented in the episode, acetylcholine is also found in the hypothalamus of aggressive people. It is therefore an accurate theory that the worm, by attaching to the hypothalamus, is making people aggressive so that acetylcholine can be produced for food. While a diet of acetylcholine is not quite the equivalent of a hearty meal of meat and potatoes, the food that some organisms survive on is surprising. Consider the simple bacterium. Normally, antibiotics kill bacteria. Some bacteria, however, find antibiotics to be quite tasty. Two hospitalized patients whose bacterial infections were treated with the antibiotic vancomycin made miraculous recoveries as soon as their antibiotic medication was stopped. Instead of killing the bacteria, the doctors were feeding them. Given this unusual example, it is perhaps less surprising that alien worms might find acetylcholine appetizing.

A brain-sucking worm that alters the behavior of its host—fact or fiction? Actually, parasites that change the behavior of their hosts to better suit their own agenda is a common theme in nature. Many parasites have complex life cycles. They spend their formative years (or days) in one host species, known as the intermediate host. To mature into an adult, they need a second host species, called the definitive host. Since the parasite must move from one host into the next, it must persuade the intermediate host to become a tasty treat for the definitive host. Since it isn't normal animal behavior to want to become somebody else's dinner, the parasite needs to change the behavior of the intermediate host by modifying its brain or central nervous system such that the hapless host doesn't mind jumping into the soup pot of the definitive host.

The choice of a tapeworm as the model for the alien worm in "Ice" makes sense scientifically. Tapeworms are masters at changing their hosts' behavior. For example, intermediate hosts for the tapeworm *Taenia multiceps* are sheep and cows; dogs and wolves are its definitive hosts. The sheep first eats the worm eggs, and the hatched larvae travel from the intestine to the brain through the bloodstream. The worm larvae then snuggle up with the sheep's brain, where they live for about seven to eight months. Sheep behave very strangely when they have larvae on the brain. They become listless and move in tight circles away from the herd. Once separated and incapacitated, the sheep are easy prey for wolves and wild dogs—the desired destination of the parasite. Since humans may also be intermediate hosts for this tapeworm, a trip to your doctor is probably in order if you are tired and have an urgent desire to walk in circles by yourself.

Another case of a parasite taking over the central nervous system of a host is that of the lancet fluke *Dicrocoelium dendriticum*. This worm has a greater dilemma than that of the canine worm just described. Its intermediate host is an ant and its definitive host is a sheep. Sheep don't normally find ants very appetizing so the worm has its work cut out trying to make sheep eat its temporary ant home. Together with a group of its buddies, an immature worm enters an ant and wriggles its way into a part of the nervous system that controls mouth parts and locomotion. The worm literally takes control of the ant's body, causing the ant to climb to the top of a blade of grass. The worm then makes the ant bite onto the tip of the grass and hang on until a sheep comes by and eats it.

If a parasite is affecting the behavior of its host, it would seem like a safe bet that it's interfering with the host's brain or central nervous system. Not true, though, for thorny-headed worms that belong to the phylum *Acanthocephala*. The intermediate host is a little aquatic crustacean called an amphipod. Amphipods normally avoid the surface of a lake as they have an understandable aversion to being eaten by predators. This all changes when they become hosts for the worms. Instead of burrowing for safety under the sand when disturbed, the confused crustaceans swim to the top of the pond. Here, they are easy prey for the definitive hosts—ducks, beavers, and muskrats. How this behavior modification occurs is a real X-File since it doesn't seem to involve either the brain or the central nervous system.

Isolated from the outside world, Scully and her fellow scientists search for a way to kill the worms without killing the human host. This job becomes even more critical when one of them, possibly Mulder, becomes infected by one of the worms. Fortunately Scully makes the dramatic and quite accidental discovery that two alien larvae will kill each other if put together in the same drop of blood. She brilliantly extrapolates that worms of a feather might not want to flock together, and two adult worms might just do each other in if introduced into a single host. This antisocial behavior of the worms puzzles one of the other scientists, for how can there be procreation in the absence of at least a little tolerance between members of the same species? The scientist is reminded that worms (at least some earthly varieties) are hermaphrodites, and can reproduce themselves in the absence of the opposite sex.

Hermaphrodite is a label given to creatures that can produce both sperm and eggs. A large number of organisms are natural hermaphrodites, including many parasites such as flukes and tapeworms, as well as some snails and fish. Animals in nine of the sixteen phyla have the anatomy and the ability to be either male or female. Some hermaphrodites live lives that even Mulder would find strange. Imagine the following opening to an *X-Files* episode: The sun rises on sunny California. Two truly gorgeous multisexed black creatures decorated with yellow and blue stripes meet each other while meandering near the beach. Sizing each other up, one creature makes the decision to eat the other. The diner grabs the dinner, and tries to suck it into its stomach. As the tension mounts, the act of cannibalism fails—dinner is just too big. So instead, the two creatures decide to have sex. The credits roll.

These "if you can't eat it have sex with it" creatures are sea slugs called *Navanax inermis*. Unless one comes upon the other from behind, they really do try to eat each other first and if that doesn't work, they have sex. Like the alien worms, the first inclination of two *Navanaxes* is to eliminate the other. Seeing as these strange slugs live in the ocean off Southern California, perhaps Mulder shouldn't be too surprised.[3]

---

[3]Well, actually, since I grew up on the sand in Malibu and the cliffs of Pacific Palisades, maybe it should be me who isn't too surprised.

It is interesting to speculate on why the hermaphroditic condition evolved in many simple animals but not in mammals or birds. Some parasites like tapeworms spend their entire life inside other organisms, living a bachelor existence while making their hosts miserable. Coming in contact with a tapeworm of the opposite sex would be problematic if only single worms can infect hosts; evolution would therefore favor the worm that was self-sufficient. Being a hermaphrodite also means that you can explore new frontiers and colonize new habitats all by yourself. However, this isn't true of all hermaphrodites. Many if not most animals that are hermaphrodites can't tango alone and therefore need another member of their species for procreation. Of course, they don't need to be too selective. Being both male and female, any other member of their species will do.

The inability to fertilize their own eggs also helps hermaphrodites avoid inbreeding. One has only to look at the Peacock clan in the *X-Files* episode "Home" to understand the dangers, both mental and physical, associated with being related at several different levels.[4] Sometimes during a single mating, hermaphrodites take turns being the male or the female, which must be an interesting experience. It was once thought that hermaphrodites lived longer than males, which would give hermaphrodites a natural selective advantage for evolutionary purposes. More recent studies, however, indicate that the males were engaging in normal macho behavior, which tended to shorten the lives of males living with other males during the experiment.

Scully's discovery that two worms will kill each other provides the answer to saving the member of the team that is infected. When an additional worm is added to the infected person, the two worms finish each other off. What then to do about the one remaining living worm? This dilemma leads to an unusual reversal of roles for our FBI heroes. Mulder wants to keep the worm alive, arguing that research is needed on its genetic structure. Scully, the scientist, wants it destroyed, feeling that the worm is too dangerous to live. The rights of species to survive often conflict with the needs of humans whose lives or livelihood demand their destruction. The eradication of poisonous snakes in the Northeastern United States, the elimination of

[4]As discussed in Chapter 3.

wolves from many parts of the country, and the destruction of the habitat of the spotted owl in the Northwestern United States are all due to conflicts between nature and man. In the end, Scully wins the argument and the worms are a threat no more.

Mighty Mites in Trees

Cutting down trees in Washington National Forest is not a job for the fainthearted. Chain saws missing their targets . . . trees crashing about . . . logs with a mind of their own . . . and if that weren't enough, loggers in the *X-Files* episode "Darkness Falls" deserve an additional measure of hazard pay for the unexpected surprise they receive after giving the final death blows to a massive old-growth tree. Unfortunately, none of them live to collect. Tiny wood mites that have made this tree their home for hundreds of years are not pleased when forced to vacate the premises after the tree tumbles to the forest floor. These little mites are not your typical wood mites. Repulsed by light and glowing a bright iridescent green, the mites soon realize that the perfect menu for those long summer days isn't dried-up tree, but rather desiccated human, conveniently wrapped in family-sized cocoons.

Radio messages to the dried-up loggers go unanswered, causing the FBI and park rangers to investigate. Mulder and Scully are shocked to discover that swarms of mites are responsible for killing the defenseless loggers. With no visible signs of UFOs or meteor impact craters, Mulder doesn't believe that the mites are the vanguard of an alien invasion. Rather, he theorizes that the mites represent a species that was probably extinct except for the inhabitants of the now dead tree. Mulder bases his views on the fact that modern-day mites aren't repulsed by light and don't glow in the dark or desiccate and cocoon hapless humans. Mulder suggests that preserved eggs of the extinct mites lay dormant beneath the ground for an untold number of years until unearthed by the eruption by a nearby volcano. Waking from their long sleep, the eggs hatched into larvae, which then crept into the tree through its roots. The mites proceeded to feast contentedly on tree innards for hundreds of years until their home was rudely toppled by the loggers.

For Mulder's theory to be within the bounds of extreme possibility, reviving other ancient eggs that are dormant and snoozing needs to be possible. The oldest eggs that have been revived are crustacean eggs laid around 1630 in a pond in Newport, Rhode Island. Sediment caused by Europeans settling in the area covered the eggs and kept them from hatching. The eggs would still be buried had not Roger Segelken of Cornell University unearthed them, which caused many of the eggs to finally hatch.

A considerable gap exists, of course, between reviving four-hundred-year-old eggs and eggs that are millions of years old. However, creatures have been brought back to life that are far older.

As a high school student, I spent many hours at the Los Angeles Museum of Natural History trying to piece together the skull of a 7-million-year-old horse (before you get too excited, it's not the horse that comes back to life). I vividly remember all those bones lying in front of me week after week like pieces from a giant three-dimensional jigsaw puzzle. It was exhausting work. Intense concentration and much trial and error led to only a few tiny fragments reuniting with neighboring bone fragments each hour. Before I began working on the horse, I thought that being a paleontologist would be exciting and fulfilling work. But after a few years of immersion in one stack of ancient bone fragments after another, I realized that being a paleontologist trainee left me with a sense of frustration. That horse was never going to trot away when completed. Nor would the ancient bones reveal many clues about the true nature of the extinct horse.

For a few scientists who study prehistoric plants and animals, these frustrations are partially assuaged by finding their tiny subjects encased in amber. Amber deposits are found all over the world, the oldest dating back some 320 million years. Sap, oozing out of wounded trees, trapped and mummified an astonishing variety of insects, crabs, scorpions, leaves, mushrooms, and even lizards. If the sap hardened in an environment where there was limited exposure to oxygen, it turned into the colorful, translucent substance known as amber. Amber provides a window into the last actions of the trapped creatures—a tiny leaf beetle preserved in the act of fighting off the sap that slowly engulfed it; a jumping spider clutching the millipede it never got a chance to eat; little fruit flies reflexively laying eggs; and midges enjoying one last romantic fling.

Browsing through the beautifully illustrated book on amber by

David Grimaldi (*Amber Window to the Past*), you can almost envision the centipedes, caterpillars, and lizards quickly scurrying up the nearest tree if released from their amber prisons. However, as lifelike as these trapped creatures look, down to the tiny scales on the wings of moths and the profuse hairs that cover the larvae of owl flies, they are, of course, very dead. These encased animals have about as much chance of coming back to life as do ancient Egyptian mummies. But what is true of the mummified animals may not be true of the tiny creatures that inhabited the insides of the dead animals. What if these endosymbionts and endopathogens are still alive, waiting only for a crack in the amber that travels through their mummified animal host to be free at last?

If these tiny creatures are still alive, then their DNA must be undamaged. The DNA of an organism is analogous to the hard drive of a computer. The DNA contains all the information required for an organism to make or acquire the substances necessary for life. Imagine how well a computer would operate if its hard drive was shattered into thousands or millions of pieces (trust me, you don't need to conduct your own experiment). Intact DNA, which is normally present as a single piece in bacterial cells, forty-six pieces in human cells, or as many as a few hundred pieces in some plant cells, is required for any organism frozen in time to restart its dormant metabolism and prepare to live again.

Scientists have been very interested in studying the DNA of organisms preserved in amber—and not simply to create living dinosaur amusement parks. By analyzing the DNA from ancestors of modern organisms, insights can be gained into the evolution of that species.

The discovery that DNA isolated from animals in amber isn't completely degraded—in other words, it isn't broken into millions of pieces—was established in 1992. Tiny fragments of DNA were sufficiently intact to be analyzed from a 25-million-year-old termite and bee. This meant that insect DNA can survive for millions of years, but apparently not in an undamaged form. The next report on ancient DNA was published in 1993, on the same day that the movie *Jurassic Park* was released. Newspaper headlines proclaimed that DNA from the time of the dinosaurs had been discovered and hinted that a real Jurassic Park might be just around the corner. The papers didn't dwell on the minor detail that the ancient DNA came from an organ-ism somewhat less exotic than Velociraptor—a weevil that inhabited the early Cretaceous period some 130 million years ago. Given the likely size of the audience for ancient-weevil amusement parks, the story soon died. However, scientific interest remains undiminished. Since then, about one third of the attempts to isolate DNA from ani-mals in amber have been successful.

The survival of even fragmented DNA from creatures trapped in amber is astonishing. Amber, being the sap of trees, is organic mate-rial composed mainly of carbon, hydrogen, and oxygen. The high oxygen content implies that the environment inside the amber is ox-idizing, which leads to the production of many free radicals that are damaging to DNA.[5] After millions of years of contact with oxygen, any DNA should be long gone. However, water is also required for DNA to fragment, and amber resin acts like a desiccant to suck water from the cells of the organisms that became trapped. The lack of wa-ter must afford some protection to the DNA and allow it to endure the millions of years of exposure to the destructive tendencies of oxygen.

Although the DNA of amber-encased weevils still is highly frag-mented, the DNA of endoparasites or endosymbionts may be much more intact. It is well known that some bacteria and fungi when pre-sented with harsh environmental conditions (such as having your host become mummified in sap) are able to form spores. Bacterial spores keep their fragile DNA in a watertight container surrounded by a thick, protective protein coat. Spores are resistant to conditions such as boiling, radiation, pressure, and chemicals that would mean instant death to an unprotected cell. Extrapolations from modern ex-periments suggest that spores could survive for several hundred thousand years if surrounded by organic material that protected their DNA from the sun's ionizing radiation, another producer of free rad-icals. Spores inside mummified insects should get plenty of protec-tion from radiation due to the organic material of the amber and the exoskeleton of the insect. However, it is a far cry from saying that spores might survive for one hundred thousand years to showing that they can survive for 25 million years.

[5]For more on free radicals and their role in disease and aging, see Chapter 5.

But this is precisely what Raul Cano from California Polytechnic State University showed in 1995. In an amazing paper published in the eminent journal *Science*, Cano described extracting bacterial spores from the insides of an extinct species of stingless bee encased in a piece of amber that was unearthed in the Dominican Republic. The spores, which Cano revived and successfully grew in the lab, were from a strain of bacteria called *Bacillus sphaericus*. This was significant, since the same bacteria live inside modern-day Dominican stingless bees.

Naturally, upon hearing the news of million-year-old bacteria growing in a lab in California, many scientists were as skeptical as Scully would have been. For this news to become truly accepted, the experiment needs to be repeated by other scientists. Unfortunately, no one except Raul Cano has been able to revive ancient bacteria, although many have tried. The skeptics prefer to believe that the little bacilli were simply contaminating modern bacteria that just happen to also live in Dominican bees and just happened to enter Cano's sterile chamber in California. These scientists will have even more reason to be skeptical when they read the most recent paper from the Cano lab. The latest work describes the isolation from amber of an ancient version of a bacterial species called *Staphylococcus*. Staphylococci don't form spores, so any revived cells must have survived for millions of years in the absence of a protective protein shell. If true, then the survival powers of DNA are much greater than previously realized.

If ordinary bacteria can be revived after snoozing for millions of years inside amber, might dormant mite eggs also survive under similar conditions? Mites are arthropods, just like spiders. At first glance, mite eggs resemble considerably smaller versions of the eggs you eat for breakfast. Crack open the shell and there's a glob of yolk inside. Mite eggs, however, come in little packets like peas in a pod, and can survive very harsh environmental conditions. If a chicken lays an egg in a hole in late fall and forgets about it, the result will be a dead, frozen chicken egg. But mites, like other land-living arthropods, have eggs that survive the winter. Arthropods make their own brand of antifreeze somewhat similar to the antifreeze used in radiators to keep car engines from freezing. Also, just like bacterial spores that must shut down their metabolism during a long sleep, mite eggs slow down their metabolic clocks when in nasty environmental conditions. In another parallel with the ancient spores, mite eggs can live in a desiccated environment. They are like cacti, able to suck water in without letting water out.

As sturdy as mite eggs are, surviving for millions of years underground protected by nothing except their waxy cuticle shell is not likely. Mulder uses brevity when reciting his theory on the origin of the mites—not too surprising given the presence of desiccated loggers hanging in trees. If he had expanded his explanation, Mulder might have speculated that the eggs survived by virtue of being encased in amber. Some of the one million different species of mites currently sharing our planet are internal parasites of insects. If an insect host became entombed in amber millions of years ago, the mites living inside the insect would suffer the same fate. Any eggs of the trapped mites would be doubly protected from the oxidizing environment of the sap and the long-term irradiation of the sun by the body of the mother mite and the insect host.

Mulder speculates that the eggs were unearthed by a volcanic eruption. Imagine a massive volcano hurling rocks, trees, and amber into the air. While it is tempting to imagine the heat of the volcano melting the amber prison, thereby releasing the trapped eggs, any temperature hot enough to melt amber would surely destroy the eggs. It's not, however, beyond the realm of extreme possibility that the amber prison was flung high into the sky by the force of a volcano and then plummeted back to Earth, slamming into the ground. The force of the impact could cause amber, mummified insect, and mother mite to shatter, releasing the stored eggs. If the eggs were still alive, they could become stimulated to begin the process of development into an embryo—perhaps they would just need some sunlight and warm temperatures; the ancient Rhode Island crustacean eggs required only a bit of fluorescent light and a few degrees above freezing to hatch from their four-hundred-year sleep. Once awakened, the mite embryos would develop into larvae, which, still groggy after such a long sleep, might climb into the nearest tree and stay hidden until their descendants are rudely disrupted hundreds of years later.

While the light-sensitive mites lie hidden throughout the day, during the night it's the humans who need to hide. As Mulder and Scully huddle in the loggers' cabin trying to will the sputtering generator to keep the single bulb lit, Scully muses on how the mites might glow in the dark. While Scully believes that the mites absorb enzymes taken from the bodies that they cocoon, there are better explanations. Fireflies glow in the dark because they can make two items: an enzyme called luciferase and a substance called luciferin. The firefly enzyme luciferase is able to make light by combining luciferin with a second substance, ATP, the fuel of cells. Humans don't make luciferase, so the mites can't be sucking this enzyme out of humans. However, humans do make and consume about four pounds of ATP every hour. It's possible that the mites make both the enzyme luciferase and the substance luciferin but not enough ATP. So maybe the mites were sucking the ATP out of human cells in order to supplement their own stores of ATP and keep glowing.

Mulder and Scully survive the night in the loggers' cabin but are attacked by the mites the following night as they try to escape from the single-minded swarms. When they are recovering in the hospital from their near fatal desiccations, a doctor tells Mulder that they found a large concentration of luciferin in their lungs, indicating that the mites probably were producing light using the enzyme luciferase. Although Mulder and Scully recover, the mites are not so fortunate. Teams of exterminators spray insecticide throughout their mountain site, wiping out the ancient swarms and returning the mites to their previous extinct state. It's doubtful that anyone, even Mulder, shed any tears over the loss of this particular species from the planet.

Life on the Rocks

INT. ENTRANCE AREA—NIGHT

MULDER

I've been going over Trepkos' work. Fragments mostly, but I found several references...to a subterranean organism.

SCULLY

What are you talking about?

MULDER

An unknown life form...existing inside the volcano.

Scully regards him skeptically, as he continues:

MULDER

I haven't found anything yet describing the organism in specific terms, but—

SCULLY

Mulder, nothing can live in the volcanic interior. Not only
because of the intense heat, but the gases would be toxic to
any organism.

MULDER

Look at this...

—"Firewalker"

You might think that an active volcano would be about the worst
place to discover the latest in new and interesting life. Surrounded by
blistering heat and toxic gases, even the most hardy organisms would
prefer more hospitable niches. Still, volcanoes don't have to contain life
to be interesting. They provide a window deep into the heart of our
planet—an opportunity to study the composition of the Earth's man-
tle, probably all that remains of the chaotic early days after planet formation. And then, of course, there is the little problem of the Earth
spewing acres of ash, lava, and gases out of volcanoes and onto devastated countryside. The worst natural disaster of the past ten thousand
years was the unexpected 1815 volcanic eruption of Tambora in In-
donesia that killed over ninety thousand people.

With over 1,500 active volcanoes, trying to predict the next catastrophic eruption falls on the shoulders of volcanologists and seismol-
ogists. These scientists use a variety of instruments to monitor the
swelling and rumblings of volcanoes prior to eruptions. To perform the
more risky jobs, the latest innovation in volcano research involves using million-dollar robots equipped with video cameras, mechanical
arms, and no sense of self-preservation. These robots descend into the

mouths of active volcanoes, take readings of the local atmosphere, and bring back the cooled remains of bubbling-hot magma—in other words, rocks. One such robot carries back rocks with an extra, added bonus to the volcanologists in the *X-Files'* episode "Firewalker": tiny hidden fungal spores. Spores that are just waiting to enter the warm and nurturing environment of a host, where they can divide and develop into a mature fungus. And human beings fit the host bill just fine.

The spores present a puzzle—how do they survive the inhospitable conditions of an active volcano? Mulder and Scully find handwritten notes from one of the volcanologists, who also has a sideline interest in slaughtering everyone in sight. The notes diagram the possible biochemistry of the unusual fungus, and suggest that the fungus's biology is based on silicon. Scully is not impressed, believing that the diagram is pure science fiction. Mulder, who has spent quite a bit of time thinking about alternative life-forms, reminds Scully that although all known life is based on carbon, silicon is the next best thing to carbon. Mulder, like many students of high school and college chemistry, probably spent hours staring at the periodic table of the elements that decorates all chemistry classrooms. His photographic memory recalls that right below carbon on the chart is silicon, meaning that silicon has properties similar to carbon. Is Scully therefore being carbocentric not to believe in the possibility of silicon-based life?

All life encountered so far relies primarily on just ten of the more than one hundred known elements: carbon, oxygen, nitrogen, hydrogen, potassium, calcium, magnesium, iron, phosphorous, and sulfur. Silicon is curiously absent from this list, even though it's the second-most-abundant Earth element by weight. Silicon makes up almost 28 percent of the total amount of elements on Earth, right behind oxygen's 47 percent. Carbon is 150 times less prevalent than silicon, at just 0.2 percent, yet it's so important to life that most molecules containing carbon are termed organic and those without carbon are called inorganic.

So why is carbon the fundamental element of life and not the much more abundant silicon? Michael Dewar and Eamonn Healy have spent even more time than Mulder pondering this question and have come up with the following support for carbon- over silicon-based life. A large number of the chemical reactions that routinely occur in all organisms release energy and are called exothermic. If a reaction releases energy, then its occurrence is favorable since the products of the chemical reaction are more stable than the original molecules that engaged in the reaction. Think of an exothermic chemical reaction as a car teetering on a precipice of a mountain. It is favorable for the car to descend to the bottom of the mountain—no energy or gas is required. The car going down the mountain gives off heat—the tires become hot in contact with the ground. The "reaction" of the car ending up on the ground is analogous to an exothermic chemical reaction.

If every possible exothermic chemical reaction in your body occurred right now, you would be starring in your own, real X-file as someone who spontaneously combusted. Fortunately, even the most exothermic reactions in your body require the presence of enzymes to help them get under way. Enzymes are proteins that help jump-start chemical reactions. That car teetering on the precipice needs a push to begin moving down the hill. Similarly, a lit match is needed to help ignite a piece of paper. Once the paper is set on fire, it will burn on its own and heat will be released. Pushing the car or touching a lit match to paper are actions analogous to those that enzymes perform. Enzymes therefore create favorable conditions so that chemical reactions can take place. Without matches, many millions of lifetimes could be spent staring at a piece of paper waiting for it to spontaneously combust. Without the proper enzyme to catalyze a chemical reaction, the reaction would also take a substantial amount of time to occur.

Silicon-based life would have to face the constant problem of spontaneous combustion. Simple carbon-based chemical reactions, such as combining carbon tetrachloride with water to generate carbon dioxide and hydrochloric acid, occur very slowly at room temperature in the absence of an enzyme catalyst. The analogous silicon-based reaction, combining silicon tetrafluoride and water, results in a violent explosion all by itself.

Such differences in the chemical reactivity of silicon and carbon are probably due to the sheer size of the silicon atom. Silicon is approximately one and one half times larger than carbon. The large size of silicon means that electrons have more room to pack around silicon during a chemical reaction than they do around the tiny carbon atom. This allows chemical reactions to occur more readily. The large size of silicon atoms would also pose a second problem for silicon-based life. Silicon organisms would be much larger than carbon-based organisms with the same number of atoms, making them heavier and not as energy efficient.

Evolution may also have bypassed silicon when designing life because of the greater variety of molecules that can form using carbon compared with silicon. Strong chemical bonds form between two atoms when they share electrons. Both carbon and silicon have four electrons available for sharing and therefore both can be tightly bonded to four different atoms. While this property allows great versatility in the number of molecules that can be formed, the smaller carbon atoms tend to form long chain molecules while silicon prefers more compact three-dimensional networks. Long chain carbon compounds play crucial roles in life. They are the fatty acids that make up the membranes that surround all cells, hormones that allow communication between cells, and vitamins that help enzymes function properly. Without the ability to form long chains of carbon—the technical term is catenation—silicon-based life would appear very different from carbon-based life.

Another reason for the popularity of carbon in living organisms is that carbon participates more easily in certain types of important chemical reactions. All the molecules of life need to be assembled from simple building blocks, much like a house is assembled from basic components like wood and glass. Some of these building blocks are carbon oxides (molecules containing carbon bonded to oxygen). These molecules can easily react with other molecules (in the presence of enzymes, of course), allowing carbons to be added or removed from molecular chains. When silicon is bonded to oxygen, it becomes glass or sand, which, as solid crystal substances, cannot participate in any further chemical reactions.

For all of these reasons, carbon-based life wins out over silicon-based life hands down. If silicon-based life developed in the same places as did carbon-based life billions of years ago, competition with carbon-based life would have soon confined silicon organisms to the evolutionary dustbin. But what about those regions of the planet that are too unpleasant for carbon-based life? Such as deep inside volcanoes? Mulder tells Scully that a silicon-based life-form in the deep biosphere is one of the holy grails of modern science. Mulder doesn't add that it would probably not be any kind of recognizable life. Scientists such as Thomas Gold at Cornell University speculate that silicon-based chemical systems not discernible as "living" may be located in regions deep within the planet, below where carbon-based life can survive. But if silicon-based life-forms exist far below the realm of carbon-based life, they would probably get passed over as just some uninteresting rock.

I am in agreement with Scully that it is highly improbable that the fungus in "Firewalker" has silicon-based biology. However, sand is left behind in the lungs of the dead volcanologists following the emergence of the fungus from its human host. How, Mulder reasons, could sand—silicon dioxide—have gotten in the lungs if the organism isn't silicon-based? An answer to Mulder's question that is less biologically earth-shattering does exist. Many organisms, both past and present, absorb silicon from the environment to make little skeletons. One class of these organisms, radiolarians, have populated the planet for about 600 million years. Radiolarians are tiny marine creatures composed of a single very large cell up to a quarter inch in diameter. Their sturdy silicon skeletons with many extruding spikes make wonderful fossils. Diatoms and silicoflagellates are other single-cell marine creatures that coat themselves with silica to form lovely little opaline silica skeletons. Like these marine creatures, the fungal spores in "Firewalker" could have absorbed silicon from their rocky home and secreted sand into the human host. While not quite as exciting as a silicon-based organism, many scientists would love to (carefully) study a fungus with such unusual properties.

While Scully works desperately to culture the fungal spores, she discovers to her relief that the spores may not survive outside a host. If this result holds up, then maybe she and Mulder aren't contaminated by being in the vicinity of the infected volcanologists and will live to solve more X-Files. Although Scully experiments by adding an undoubtedly delicious broth of human tissue, blood, saliva, and sulfur to the spore's new test tube home, they still stubbornly refuse to grow.

Scientifically, this is a very accurate picture of endoparasites, that class of organisms that spend their lives inside other organisms. It's notoriously difficult to find the right mix of ingredients and environmental conditions to make endoparasites thrive outside their hosts. Scully hypothesizes that the spores must be inhaled immediately after the mature fungus rips through the neck of its previous human host. This hypothesis, while comforting to the uninfected, might not be accurate. The spores could still be alive and infectious and just not willing to grow in a test tube. After all, the spores are able to survive inside a rock deep within a volcano until a new home comes along. The only scientific way to make sure that the released spores are harmless is to try and use them to infect another person. Any volunteers?

Then again, maybe Scully is correct and the spores cannot live outside a host. An organism more used to the typical volcanic gases of water vapor, carbon dioxide, and sulfur dioxide might find the oxygen in the air to be toxic. About half of all known life on Earth can live without oxygen. For some of these creatures, most of which are bacteria, even the slightest trace of oxygen is toxic. Other microbes are more nonchalant about oxygen—if it's around they will use it; if not, they live happily without it. Higher organisms like animals have no choice. You, for example, will breathe in oxygen about 8 million times this year. As the old adage goes, "In comes the good air, out goes the bad air." Oxygen comes in, and carbon dioxide goes out. The oxygen inhaled is used for a specific purpose—to make ATP, the fuel molecule of the cell. A rather complicated series of chemical reactions take place in all cells involving the transfer of electrons from one molecule to another, like an old-fashioned fire brigade transferring pails of water from one person to the next. The final molecule that accepts the electrons is oxygen, which then combines with two hydrogen ions to form water. The oxygen you breathe in is therefore converted into water. This process is coupled (in a way not completely understood) to the making of ATP. The electrons that get handed over to oxygen originate from the food you eat, which is how food is used for fuel. The carbon dioxide exhaled is produced as a by-product of many different chemical reactions that take place in cells and is not directly related to the oxygen inhaled.

Oxygen makes up 21 percent of the atmosphere, but this wasn't always true. Oxygen first appeared 3.5 billion years ago as a highly toxic waste product of a newfangled process called photosynthesis. It took about a billion years for oxygen to become plentiful in the air, thanks to photosynthesizing plants like algae. Besides rusting out the rocks on the planet's surface, oxygen wiped out any microbe that couldn't handle its destructive forces. Those that survived produced enzymes that could neutralize the effects of oxygen or were buried deep underground where oxygen from the surface couldn't penetrate. In the fungal spores in "Firewalker" are allergic to oxygen, they would certainly die in the air unless inhaled quickly by a convenient host.

"Firewalker" ends with Mulder and Scully enjoying a month-long vacation in a level 4 decontamination chamber designed to make quite sure that they were not infected with the lethal fungus. This facility, called the Slammer, is real and is located at Fort Detrick in Maryland. With just enough beds for Mulder and Scully, accommodations include epoxy-sealed cement walls, individual bathrooms, a window that overlooks a grassy courtyard, and a special air supply that is exchanged fifteen times hourly. The staff wait on guests in full space suit regalia and must take decontamination showers and step into an ultraviolet light box when entering and leaving. To reserve free accommodations in such luxurious, and no doubt enormously expensive surroundings, one needs only to become infected with Ebola or Lassa fever viruses or deadly fungal spores from volcanic rocks or alien Alaskan worms.

It's a vacation spot that people are, literally, dying to get into.

Fungi, Fungi, Everywhere

INT N.D. SEDAN

                        SCULLY
Did he tell you what happened?

                        MULDER
Flash of light, yellow rain, Maria, Maria!

Scully looks at him, unsure of him for a moment.

                        SCULLY
He didn't kill her, Mulder.

Mulder gives her a questioning look.

SCULLY

I examined the body of Maria Dorantes and believe the cause
of death was natural, if not strange. She seems to have suc-
cumbed to a massive fungal infection.

MULDER

A fungus?

—"El Mundo Gira"

Migrant workers in the San Joaquin Valley of central California
have many worries—exploitive employers, immigration officers, exposure to pesticides . . . and El Chupacabra, the legendary goatsucker. In the *X-Files'* episode *"El Mundo Gira,"* the Buente brothers,
Eladio and Soledad, have problems that are more mundane. Both
have fallen in love with Maria, a fetching young woman who takes
care of the goats. Suddenly, a bright light flashes and hot yellow rain
descends from a cloudless sky. A goat and Maria, her face eaten away,
are found dead in a nearby field. Eladio, the brother with Maria at
the time of the unusual downpour, suspiciously flees the scene.

Mulder brings a reluctant Scully to investigate the slayings, saying that he is intrigued by the yellow rain, since rainstorms with interesting tints are linked to alien encounters. Scully prefers to believe
that the deaths are more prosaic; Eladio must have killed Maria since
she preferred his brother. Scully doesn't speculate on who killed the
goat. A third theory is espoused by an older woman at the camp:
Maria and the goat were killed by El Chupacabra, a mythical four-
foot-tall creature with red eyes, fangs, and gray skin that revels in
sucking the blood out of livestock and pets.

Scully revises her original hypothesis when she sees that the
body of Maria is blanketed with a green-gray fungus. And not an
alien, mutant, buried-in-a-rock-near-a-meteorite fungus. Just simple, ordinary *Aspergillus,* a brown mold so useful to humans yet so
harmful as well. Scully is probably aware that when enjoying a refreshing soft drink, she is drinking citric acid produced by vats of the
Aspergillus mold. A different species of *Aspergillus* is used to give soy

sauce its tangy fermented flavor. Scully is correct when she tells Mulder that *Aspergillus* is everywhere—in compost and dead leaves, on walls and in household dust. Start an air conditioner in the summer and thousands of *Aspergillus* spores blow out of the vents.

Aspergillus is a scourge of crop plants, especially corn and peanuts. The warnings about not eating peanuts with any sign of mold are given for good reason. *Aspergillus* that infects peanut plants can produce a cancer-causing substance called aflatoxin. Aflatoxin was discovered in England in the 1960s during a turkey disease epidemic. Turkeys were dying and no one could come up with a reasonable cause. The so-called "Turkey X disease" turned out to be caused by an *Aspergillus* contamination of the peanut meal fed to the turkeys. There was so much aflatoxin in some batches of ground peanuts that the poor turkeys were dropping like flies.

Scully tells Mulder that *Aspergillus*, while normally harmless to humans, can be occasionally dangerous, especially when infecting people with weakened immune systems. Every day, your body fights an invisible battle with billions of disease agents like bacteria, viruses, fungi, and protozoa—pathogens that aren't interested in peaceful coexistence. Most of the battles are won since evolution has favored people with top-notch defenses. Some of your defenses work against all types of potential intruders. The defensive system known as the skin is your castle wall. Keep it intact and you stand a good chance of keeping the enemy out. If the wall is breached by a cut or splinter then the enemy gleefully marches in. Of course the enemy can enter through eye or nose doorways or through that great portcullis called a mouth. A castle wouldn't leave such obvious entryways unguarded, and neither does the body. Each of these entries has additional defenses. Tear ducts secrete an enzyme called lysozyme that breaks apart invading cells like bacteria and protozoa. The mucous membranes in the nose trap foreign invaders and secrete lysozyme as a backup defense. What you eat goes into the stomach, an environment not friendly to pathogens. Next time you get annoyed at acid indigestion, think about what that acid is doing to the enemies within.

Even the most secure castle needs mobile defenders, which are plentiful thanks to your immune system. Some of these defenders will respond to anything they think is an enemy without caring who the enemy is. These are the white blood cells called macrophages ("big eaters") that devour invaders whole. At the site of a breach in the skin caused, for example, by a cut or a splinter, an inflammation battle rages. Some injured skin cells fight the invading hordes by making the chemical substance histamine. Histamine enlarges local blood vessels, allowing more blood to race to the site bringing along those hungry macrophages. Extra blood also heats up the region, making the site less hospitable for the enemy microbes to colonize.

If these steps are unsuccessful in repulsing the invasion, 7 trillion elite castle warriors are ready and willing to spring into action. These are the white blood cells called lymphocytes. Lymphocytes come in two classes, T-cells and B-cells. Like all white blood cells, T-cells and B-cells are born inside bones. Immature T-cells learn their battle skills in the thymus (hence the appellation "T"), which in humans is located near the heart. Mature T-cells emerge from the thymus covered with receptor proteins on their surface in an almost infinite variety of puzzle piece–like shapes. The receptors on each individual T-cell are identical; different T-cells have different receptors. If an invading microbe or virus has a protein puzzle piece on its surface that happens to fit into one of the receptor puzzle pieces on a T-cell, the T-cell can turn into a killer cell, spelling doom for the invaders.

Some T-cells don't become killers themselves but instead help their B-cell cousins. B-cells were first identified in the bursa of fabricius (hence the term "B"), an anatomical structure found in birds. B-cells also contain a seemingly infinite variety of receptors on their surface. When the receptor on a B-cell makes a perfect fit with the puzzle piece on the surface of an invader, then that B-cell reproduces itself into an army of identical B-cell warriors. The warriors fight with weapons called antibodies, which the B-cells make and spit out into the bloodstream at the rate of two thousand antibody molecules each second. The antibodies are like loose puzzle pieces with two sides that each can fit with the corresponding puzzle piece on the surface of the invading pathogen. If the antibodies floating around in the bloodstream bump into the enemy, they form clumps with the pathogen, providing a delicious meal for the macrophages. Some of the activated B-cells become memory cells. Years later, if the memory cell encounters the original puzzle piece on a pathogen trying once again to invade, they can quickly spring into action. This is how vaccines work. Disabled pathogens are provided to your immune system in advance, stimulating production of memory cells and making your body ready for when a real attack takes place.

Sometimes it seems as if the immune system has switched sides and joined the enemy. Allergic reactions occur when some harmless substance like dust, pollen, or feline saliva on cat hair triggers a massive and unneeded immune response. The surfaces of these common materials can resemble puzzle pieces that the immune system is primed to respond to. The body initiates a substantial and unnecessary counterattack, complete with T-cells, inflammation, increased histamine levels, and dilation of blood vessels. If only the nose is affected, it's called hay fever. If it involves the lungs, it's asthma. The immune system can also fail to distinguish cells that belong to a person's own tissues and those which are enemy cells. Autoimmune disorders are diseases in which the immune system turns traitor and attacks the body's own cells. Almost 2 million people in the United States are living with lupus, a disease in which the immune system attacks the skin, kidneys, lungs, heart, and brain. Muscle cells are the unwitting target in myasthenia gravis, another immune disorder.

Scully tells Mulder that people with weakened immune systems, who are referred to as immunocompromised, are particularly at risk for infection by any potential disease agents and this may be why Maria died from simple *Aspergillus*. If Maria has a depressed immune system, then the castle that is her body has few defenders. If this is true, then when a potentially dangerous organism like *Aspergillus* bypasses the castle wall, it's free to colonize at will. One of today's frightening realities is that more and more people have weakened immune systems, which is contributing to an explosion of diseases caused by bacteria, fungi, and viruses. In the United States alone, more than 120 billion dollars are spent each year on the treatment of infectious diseases. Between 1980 and 1992, deaths from infectious diseases rose 22 percent, not including the AIDS epidemic.

Maria could have become immunocompromised in one of three ways. First, she could have been born that way. A very small percentage of people have inherited a weak immune system and are naturally more susceptible to infections. Second, she could be infected with the human immunodeficiency virus (HIV), which accounts for a substantial number of people with weakened immune systems. HIV is so deadly because it attacks T-cells, the very system created to combat viruses. Third, Maria could have been exposed to, or treated with, a compound that suppresses her immune system. People who are undergoing chemotherapy or organ transplantation are given chemicals or treated with radiation that temporarily suppresses the body's natural immune responses.

If Maria's immune system was compromised, then a fungus that is normally harmless like *Aspergillus* could have invaded her sinuses and caused a lethal form of meningitis or it could have colonized her lungs, also with fatal results. Scully speculates that Maria's immune system may have been damaged by exposure to high levels of the pesticide methyl bromide. With 27,000 tons of methyl bromide dumped on United States soil each year, exposure of farm workers is a major health problem. Use of methyl bromide also has a second side effect—it causes massive depletion of the ozone layer. Since the ozone layer is all that stands between the sun's UV radiation and people riddled with wrinkles and skin cancer, the Environmental Protection Agency has decided to phase out the production and import of methyl bromide (but not its use) starting in 2001.

However, methyl bromide exposure turns out to be a false trail: regardless of the levels of the chemical in Maria's blood, the prodigious amounts of *Aspergillus* in her system would have been deadly even without a compromised immune system.

Maria is not the only victim of normally innocuous fungi. All the victims have one common denominator: they all came in contact with Eladio. When Scully consults an expert on fungi, known as a mycologist, she learns of a man killed by a dermatophyte, a fungus that causes the relatively harmless but annoying malady of athlete's foot. Apparently, something or someone is causing "harmless" fungi to grow at hundreds of times their normal rates, allowing lethal levels to contact people. The scientist shows Scully an unusual enzyme that he has isolated from several of the speedy fungi, an enzyme that just happens to be the same color as the original yellow rain. When he adds a pinch of the enzyme to *Puccinia graminis*, the fungus that causes the widespread crop disease black stem rust, the fungus immediately starts overflowing its container. The scientist's conclusion: the strange, yellow-colored enzyme accelerates the growth of fungi. The mycologist and Scully are horrified by the implications of an enzyme that turns common fungi into dangerous pathogens. Fungi are everywhere, on everything and everyone. As a scientist, Scully knows that life on this planet won't survive if faced with the prospect of runaway fungus growth.

The growth of fungi at the rate depicted by the mycologist in *"El Mundo Gira"* is pure science fiction. For fungal cells or any other cells to divide, they first need to double all the items in the cell. This means that all the proteins, sugars, DNA, lipids, and other cellular molecules must be duplicated before cell division can begin. In this way, when one cell divides into two, the two daughter cells will be virtual copies of the parent cell. Even the simplest cells, those belonging to bacteria, take about twenty minutes to crank out another set of everything before dividing. The fungus yeast, without which bread couldn't rise, takes a bit longer than bacteria to divide. The supercharged fungi in *"El Mundo Gira"* are dividing in less than milliseconds. It's great science fiction but not quite real science.

Mulder believes that the yellow enzyme being unconsciously spread by Eladio is of alien origin. Since no earthly enzyme can speed up cell division to such an extent, he is probably correct. When Chris Carter calls and asks me to come up with real science to explain some aspect of a story line, I always keep in mind the mantra of science fiction: aliens can do almost anything. So maybe alien enzymes can speed up fungal growth by speeding up how fast the fungal cells can divide. While not my idea, it is not outside the realm of remote possibility.

So how might such an enzyme speed up a cell's ability to divide? One way is for the enzyme to make cells want to divide. Proteins called growth factors cause cells to start immediate preparations for doubling in size and then splitting in half. Growth factors are naturally involved in healing wounds. When you cut yourself deep enough to bleed, the cut doesn't stay open for very long. Tiny cell fragments called platelets that float around in the bloodstream soon arrive on the scene. These platelets release a protein called platelet-derived growth factor. Skin cells contain a receptor for the growth factor protein. When the growth factor joins with the receptor on the surface of a cell in the neighborhood of a cut, the cell is stimulated to start dividing to make more cells that will close the gap caused by the wound. If the alien enzyme functions like a growth factor, fungal cells that normally might be nonchalant about dividing would get the message to start cranking out more cells ASAP.

How quickly a cell can divide depends mainly on how fast it can duplicate its DNA. DNA is made up of two chains that wind around each other—the famous double helix. Regions of the DNA known as "origins of replication" are places where the two chains separate from each other, which forms a local bubble in the DNA. The regions where the chains separate provide spaces for special enzymes, called polymerases, to interact with the DNA and start the duplication process. The more origins of replication, the more enzymes can get their hands on the DNA and start doing their job. If the alien enzyme is able to establish millions of additional origins of replication, the time required to duplicate DNA would be measured in seconds, not minutes. Cell division would be more rapid than normal—but still not fast enough. There is a maximum speed that enzymes can work at to complete the tasks of duplicating a cell's ingredients prior to the cell dividing in two. Enzymes are like little molecular machines, and like all machines that have to physically join components together or break them into pieces, there is some maximum speed at which they work. To make any machine work faster, it must be reengineered. Therefore, the alien enzyme would have to modify hundreds, if not thousands, of enzymes in the fungus to speed up cell division to the extent portrayed in the episode.

But, then, aliens can do almost anything.

Mulder theorizes that the yellow enzyme came to Earth on a meteorite. The meteorite could have plummeted through the atmosphere, creating the bright lights seen by the migrant workers. Mulder speculates that if the meteor smashed into a body of water near the migrant camp, scalding water and concentrated enzyme could have rained down upon Eladio, Maria, and the goat. Meteorites like this fictional one have been crashing into the Earth since the original formation of the planet. Hundreds of tons of meteoroids, the name given to meteorites while they are still hurling through space, enter the atmosphere every day. Thankfully, most are small and burn up before reaching the ground. The ones that land, while detrimental to life and limb of those unfortunate to be in the immediate vicinity, are scientifically fascinating as they provide firsthand evidence of the composition of other planets and comets.

Could an alien enzyme have traveled through space on meteoroids as speculated by Mulder? Most enzymes are proteins, and proteins are made up of chains of molecular beads called amino acids. Extraterrestrial amino acids have been found on meteorites, such as the famous Murchison meterorite of Australia, which fell to Earth on September 28, 1969. Residents reported hearing a crackling and hissing sound, while bright orange and red lights filled the sky. The charcoal-black Murchison meteorite then touched down at supersonic speed and splattered all over the tranquil Aussie landscape. The chemical nature of the Murchison meteorite indicates that it may have been the remnant of a spent comet. Just where it acquired its amino acids isn't known.

Meteorites are sorted into three major groups: iron, stony, and ones that are part iron, part stony. Meteorites that are just iron or stone, while interesting to geologists, barely cause a biologist to raise an eyebrow. However, a subset of the stony meteorites are called carbonaceous chondrites because they contain small rounded bodies called chondrules. These meteorites are filled with complex, carbon-containing molecules, including amino acids. All earthly proteins are constructed from twenty different amino acids. The Murchison meteorite contains some of the common earthly amino acids but also other amino acids that are rare or never-before found. The amino acids in the meteorite are in single units, not joined together as in proteins. Nonetheless, if amino acids can survive a trip through space on a meteoroid, it is not a great leap to wonder if proteins could survive as well. The mycologist tells Scully that the enzyme he has isolated is like no other. He may have been referring to the amino acid composition of the protein. If nonearthly amino acids are in the enzyme, its extraterrestrial origin could be nearly guaranteed.

For some reason, the yellow alien enzyme isn't speeding up the growth of fungi on Eladio. Instead, he is a carrier, a Typhoid Mary, spreading the enzyme and its lethal effects wherever he goes. Typhoid Mary is a general term given to people who, although exhibiting few symptoms themselves, can spread a communicable disease. The original Typhoid Mary was Mary Mallon, an Irish immigrant cook. Between 1900 and 1907, over one hundred New Yorkers became infected with *Salmonella typhosa*, the bacteria that cause typhoid, by eating Mary's less-than-sanitary cooking. Several died. Mary was a threat because she refused to stop working as a cook. Every time a new outbreak of typhoid was discovered, there was Mary cooking for the victims. Exasperated city officials finally banished her to a hospital on a Manhattan island, where she languished involuntarily for thirty years. Today, typhoid carriers must register with local health departments and are not allowed to work as food handlers. Unfortunately, the bacteria they are infected with cannot be eliminated with antibiotics.

"El Mundo Gira" is a story of creatures hidden under our very noses that emerge from obscurity to become deadly pathogens. This is not science fiction. Whether or not a new organism will suddenly be found that causes sickness and death depends on a number of factors. Has the organism acquired new abilities to infect people because it has mutated? Have new ways been found for the organism to come in contact with people? The fungi in "El Mundo Gira" emerge from obscurity because they grow so quickly that the host's immune system is unable to stop the infection. The fungi are transmitted because a carrier, Eladio, is able to spread the enzyme that causes the fungi to become so deadly. This is, in many ways, similar to how real emerging pathogens develop.

Eladio and his brother, their faces increasingly covered in fungus that makes them look like humanoid monsters, are not exiled to a hospital like Typhoid Mary. Rather, at the end of the episode, the Buente brothers are seen walking in the direction of their native Mexico. Perhaps their marred appearances will keep them hidden away and therefore unable to inadvertently kill more people. And maybe people who are spared by their self-exile will glimpse them on occasion, and mistake the brothers for El Chupacabra, giving people like Mulder plenty to do in the years ahead.

Bugging the Rain Forests

EXT. RAIN FOREST—NIGHT

As CAMERA PANS a one-man camp, a long extinguished fire, pup tent, we hear a BURST of radio static, then a faint, trembling voice:

DR. TORRENCE (O.S.)

RBP Field Base, come in. Field Base, come in please.

FINDING DR. TORRENCE

slumped weakly against a log in his one-man camp, talking into his radio mike. His flashlight illuminates his sweat-soaked face covered with large, angry BOILS. He is deathly ill.

DR. TORRENCE

This is Dr. Robert Torrence, with the Biodiversity Project, requesting immediate evacuation from sector zee-one-five...

CAMERA PUSHES IN uncomfortably close on Dr. Torrence. The spill from the flashlight casts shadows on his face, making its already grotesque contours appear even more macabre.

DR. TORRENCE

This is a medical emergency. Please respond.

—"F. Emasculata"

Without tropical willow leaves there would be no aspirin. Without the Australian rain forest there would be no corkwood trees and therefore no scopolamine to ease the queasiness of motion sickness. Without the cinchona tree, there would be no quinine to treat malaria. Without tropical plants, there would be no chocolate, coffee, or ice cream. Animals, plants, and fungi are filled with natural products that provide rubber for tires, sweets for palates, and treatments for illnesses. About half of the world's medicinal drugs originated in wild plants. Of the 50 million different organisms that exist on Earth, fewer than 2 million have been identified. Many of the unidentified organisms lie hidden in the dense, wet forests of the tropics.

It is no wonder then that entomologist Dr. Robert Torrence in the *X-Files'* episode *"F. Emasculata"* is slogging through the vast Costa Rican rain forest looking for exotic insects for his employer, Pinck Pharmaceuticals. Rain forests are overflowing with the largest assortment of insects anywhere on the planet. Insects are everywhere— flying though tree canopies so dense that little light reaches the ground, buzzing at eye level under the green mossy layers that blanket trees, and scurrying along the deeply weathered soil of the forest floor. And, let's not forget about the really cool insects crawling around inside dead pigs. Not even large purple, pulsating pig boils spewing out gooey liquid can keep Dr. Torrence from capturing a new insect species—*Faciphaga emasculata*. After sending the promising little bug back to the home company, Dr. Torrence finds himself afflicted with the same ailment as the pig, and experiencing the same fatal symptoms.

Although the Pinck pharmaceutical company is fictitious, all major pharmaceutical companies have teams scouring remote rain forests for interesting new species of plants and animals. Insects like the one captured by the late Dr. Torrence are returned to company labs, where samples of mashed-up bugs are tested to see if they contain any chemicals with possible therapeutic properties. For example, Pinck Pharmaceuticals scientists may have added *F. emasculata* extracts to cells infected with HIV, the virus that causes AIDS, to determine if something in the extract kills infected cells while leaving uninfected cells unharmed. If the scientists are lucky and find that only infected cells die after the treatment, then they need to determine which of the thousands of chemicals inside the bug mash is having the desired effect. The chemical might be anything—a protein, sugar, lipid, or maybe some other cellular molecule. Once the chemical is identified, the scientists search for unwanted side effects. For example, if the miracle HIV-destroying chemical also causes cells to become cancerous, the cure would be worse than the illness.

Next come extensive animal trials where other side effects can emerge, like purple pulsing oozing pustules. If all goes well (and it rarely does), approval can be requested from the United States Food and Drug Administration for the first human tests. Volunteers are given doses that are minuscule at first, then slowly increased. If side effects are still minimal, clinical trials begin to determine if the chemical has any therapeutic effect on people who are sick. If the answer is yes, then a new drug is ready for final approval and marketing. If the answer is no, then a considerable amount of money has been wasted. On average, the process for the discovery and development of a single drug takes about twelve years and 230 million dollars. The number of drugs that fail along the way far outnumber the drugs that are finally brought to market.

The unscrupulous Pinck Pharmaceuticals determines that *F. emasculata* contains an interesting dilating agent that could help prevent heart disease by opening up clogged blood vessels. Hoping to save a few hundred million dollars, the company decides to forgo the time-consuming and expensive process of purifying the active chemical and testing it on animals. After all, if the chemical is harmful to humans, millions of dollars will be saved by skipping the initial steps. Since enthusiastic volunteers willing to be exposed to *F. emasculata* aren't lining up at company headquarters, an anonymous package containing a dead pig leg crawling with insects is sent to a prisoner at a correction facility. Soon, a contagion is spreading out of control at the prison.

When two of the infected prisoners escape, Mulder and Scully are called in to help in their recapture. When they arrive at the prison, they find not only dying prisoners, but a decontamination crew busily burning everything in sight—including evidence needed for their investigation. One of the accidentally afflicted is Pinck Pharmaceuticals scientist Dr. Osbourne, who informs Scully that the insect itself isn't harmful; rather the bug contains an internal guest called a parasitoid, and it is the parasitoid that is causing the disease.

Parasitoids aren't exactly predators or parasites. Predators are animals that eat living organisms but prefer to live outside their prey. Parasites are much smaller than the organisms they attack. They can live inside or outside their host and don't necessarily kill it. Parasitoids are very large parasites that spend at least part of their lives inside their hosts, which they eventually kill by eating its innards. The most common parasitoids are wasps, which lay their eggs inside insect eggs. The wasp eggs hatch into larvae that eat through the larvae of their insect host.

F. emasculata is not the only *X-Files* episode that uses parasites or parasitoids in the plot. The worm in the episode "Ice" would probably be classified as a parasite, since it doesn't directly kill the host. In "Firewalker," the large fungus that derives nourishment from its human hosts and kills them as part of its life cycle could be considered a parasitoid. Parasites play an important role in the plot of "Never Again." People tattooed in the episode, including Scully, suffer from a condition called ergotism, characterized by hallucinations and mood alterations. It turns out that the ink used for the tattoos is made from rye plants that are contaminated with the fungal parasite ergot. Since the hallucinogen LSD is made from ergot, it's understandable that people exposed to ergot see objects that don't necessarily exist. In the Middle Ages, mass poisonings by ergot were common whenever the growing season was cool and wet enough to cause grains like rye, wheat, and barley to become covered with the fungus. Linnda Caporael, a professor of psychology at Rensselaer Polytechnic Institute, believes that the women accused of being witches in Salem, Massachusetts, in 1692 were not possessed by the devil, merely stoned on rye that was infected with ergot. In modern times, ergot has become a major problem by parasitizing sorghum grain, which is fed to pigs and cows. While it is difficult to determine if the animals suffer from hallucinations, they don't like to eat or produce milk while under the influence.

Dr. Osbourne tells Scully that the *F. emasculata* larvae containing the parasitoid make their way into humans through nasal or eye cavities. The parasitoid then produces a toxin that causes the oozing, pulsating boils and lesions. This fictitious disease is remarkably similar to a real disease called myiasis (from the Greek word *myia*, which means "fly"). Myiasis is caused by the invasion of body tissues or cavities by the larvae of insects such as the human botfly (*Dermatobia hominus*), which is found in Central and South America. Victims commonly return from a visit to these areas with what appears to be either nasty boils, infected skin abscesses, or insect bites. Underneath the skin, though, the botfly larvae crawl.[6]

Within weeks of leaving Central or South America, botfly victims find the first purplish lesions on their skin. Then, like *F. emasculata* crawling out of the pig lesions, mature botfly larvae wriggle out of real lesions. Sometimes, instead of emerging, they merely peek out, appearing to some sufferers like "tiny white things with black eyes." The standard treatment if you're suffering from an invasion of the botflies is to apply raw meat or pork fat to the lesion to draw the larvae out. In the United States, the meat used is bacon and the technique is referred to as "bacon therapy." In a paper published by *The Journal of the American Medical Association,* Timothy Brewer and his col-

---

[6]This is remarkably like the behavior of certain alien worms, first discovered in Alaska by a group of geophysicists.

leagues describe how after covering the lesion with bacon for about three hours, the bacon must be removed slowly to keep the larvae from scurrying back into "the safety of their subcutaneous lair."

The main problem in treating myiasis is convincing patients not to manually extract the larvae at home—crushing the larvae while still under the skin can lead to an infection. Sometimes patients suffering from myiasis are misdiagnosed as having a mental disorder. Imagine the conversation—"Doctor, I feel like I have insects crawling around under my skin!" Based on the titles of articles they publish in medical journals, doctors that treat myiasis patients must have a sense of humor. Some favorites are: "An unexpected surprise in a common boil"; "*Dermatobia hominis* in the accident and emergency department: 'I've got you under my skin' "; and "Souvenirs from Belize: the botfly and the screwworm fly." Thankfully, botfly larvae don't contain any toxic parasitoids so human hosts recover rapidly after bug extraction.

While Scully is helping Dr. Osbourne find ways of controlling the contagion, he explains to her that the parasitoid is undetectable in the human bloodstream and therefore is probably unable to reproduce outside its insect host. Since the growth and reproduction of a parasitoid is normally limited to one specific host, it is not surprising that the parasitoid reproduces only while inside *F. emasculata*. The test devised by Dr. Osbourne to determine if a person is infected (prior, of course, to the appearance of purple pustules on the skin) is to let uninfected insects suck on a person's blood for thirty minutes. If any parasitoid larvae are transmitted to the insects then the person must be infected. Scientifically, this seems like an appropriate although unnerving experiment that Scully has to perform on herself.

The emergence of dangerous disease agents from the rain forests is not simply a threat on *The X-Files*. Ecological changes due to dams and deforestation have led to new diseases such as Rift Valley fever and Argentine hemorrhagic fever. Humans for the first time are coming in contact with animals infected with exotic diseases, as did the entomologist in "F. emasculata." Many such animals are infected with viruses that find human hosts much to their taste. The Evandro Chagas Institute in Belém, Brazil, has recently isolated more than 183 new arboviruses, which are transmitted by mosquitoes, fleas, ticks, or lice and can cause deadly infections in humans.

The organization in the United States that is called in when deadly new diseases emerge is the CDC, with its nearly seven thousand people in 170 occupations. The CDC has recently increased its activities in the field of emerging pathogens as a result of recent outbreaks of a new strain of hantavirus in the Southwestern United States in 1993 and the Ebola virus in Africa in 1995. With old and new infectious diseases breaking out around the world, and modern travel breaking down the traditional boundaries of oceans and mountains, the role of the CDC as sentry and doorkeeper is becoming increasingly important.

The pneumonic plague outbreak in India in 1995 showed how the CDC springs into action. While plague cases are rare in the United States, up to forty people each year in Western states are still stricken with the disease. All three types of plague—bubonic, septicemic, and pneumonic—are caused by the *Yersinia pestis* bacterium, which lies hidden in rodents and is transmitted to humans by fleas. Pneumonic plague, a Class 1 internationally quarantinable disease, has the additional distinction of being transmitted through the air. If you incautiously spend time around a person with pneumonic plague, in one to three days you will come down with a high fever and start coughing up blood. Soon, pneumonia will set in, making breathing difficult. If antibiotic treatments are not begun within twenty-four hours of first contact, death is as certain today as it was in the Middle Ages.

The last major outbreak of pneumonic plague in the United States took place in Los Angeles in 1924. A Mexican woman and eighteen of her friends died within a few days of one another from severe pneumonia. Soon afterward, the diagnosis of plague was made. By the time the last rat in the neighborhood had been eliminated, thirty of thirty-two people infected with the bacteria had died. With this outbreak in mind, the CDC paid close attention when in late August 1994, health officials in India reported the first cases of bubonic plague, which sometimes precedes pneumonic plague. By September, over three hundred unconfirmed cases of pneumonic plague and thirty-six deaths were reported in the Indian city of Surat. Two million terrified residents fled the area, bringing the plague to other cities, including Bombay and New Delhi. Countries across the globe started panicking, with some closing their borders to Indian travelers and discontinuing flights to and from India.

The CDC, unwilling to make a pariah out of an entire country, engaged in its own course of action. The game plan involved writing articles and documents for distribution to public health officials and agencies informing them of the dangers and symptoms of pneumonic plague. The media also became involved, and a special plague hotline telephone number was created. All airline passengers coming from India were given information cards that described signs and symptoms of the plague. Physicians were contracted to serve as quarantine officers at all major airports. It was a bad time to feel queasy on a transatlantic flight since flight attendants reported any sick passengers, all of whom were whisked away to hospitals on landing. Passengers seated nearby were also put on antibiotics. In the thirty days that the surveillance was in place, thirteen airline travelers were examined, none of whom had the plague.

While it is common to think that emerging diseases originate in faraway places like the Costa Rican rain forest before they travel to the United States, the opposite can also be true. In 1995, a woman from Seattle was infected while in East Africa with a disease caused by *Hermetia illucens*, the black soldier fly. This was unusual in two respects. First, *H. illucens* was not known to infect living humans, preferring instead rotting corpses, fruits, and vegetables. Second, black soldier flies are found primarily in Florida and California and were introduced inadvertently into Africa.

Mulder and Scully are hard on the trail of the escaped prisoners, who pose a public health hazard every bit as serious as the plague. Since *F. emasculata* is transmitted by simply contacting the pus oozing from the boils, everyone who comes in contact with the prisoner, including his girlfriend, is exposed. Thanks to the efforts of Mulder and Scully, widespread deaths are averted when the prisoner is cornered and killed before he can infect a bus filled with people. One can only imagine the repercussions at Pinck Pharmaceuticals when the inevitable hordes of CDC, FDA, and FBI agents invade their slimy operations. As all real pharmaceutical companies are well aware, government regulations on new drug development are in place for good reasons. For one never knows who will bring back the next innocuous insect from the heart of some exotic place that has a nasty little guest inside looking to step up to new and better hosts.

2

Visitors from the Void

Introduction

June 8, 2008, 9:46 A.M.; Fort Detrick, Maryland.

Four scientists garbed in bulky space suits sit clustered around an electron microscope in a sterile, BL4 top containment room. Three of the scientists watch intensely as the project director carefully places a drop of amber liquid from a test tube onto a grid. Inside the test tube are microscopic cells removed days earlier from the surface of a nondescript reddish rock—a rock like many that lie scattered along desert roadways. But the desert this rock came from lies 50 million miles from the nearest road.

The scientists are visibly nervous. They had accepted the current dogma that samples retrieved from the surface of Mars contain no living matter. The Martian atmosphere, only 1 percent that of sister planet Earth, doesn't protect the rocky surface from the intense ultraviolet radiation of the distant sun. Water, in its liquid form so necessary for life, exists at the frigid Martian surface only as ice, and even the ice is restricted to the polar caps. Life might be found by drilling deep below the Martian surface, to where water is liquid and kilometers of rock afford protection from the harsh surface conditions. This kind of deep drilling necessitates the presence of man, and landing men on Mars is still only a paper fantasy. Life shouldn't be found on surface rocks that can be retrieved by robots, yet here they are in the room, waiting and wondering.

The director finishes preparing the specimen for viewing and inserts the grid into the vacuum chamber of the powerful scanning electron microscope. The eyes of all the scientists focus on the microscope's video monitor. The seconds that pass waiting for the image to come into focus seem like years. And the wait *has* been years. Four years in preparation for the Mars Surveyor 2001 mission. Months spent waiting for the ship to make the giant leap across interplanetary space. More time for the rover with its Athena instrument payload to obtain core samples from within surface rocks, and for the samples to be launched into orbit. And then years waiting for the Mars Sample Return Ship to dock with the orbiting sample container and ferry the precious rocks back to Earth. Finally, after all this time, more waiting while old arguments were revisited about the need for additional precautions to protect Earth from imaginary hordes of deadly alien microbes—a scenario expounded by nervous politicians who grew up on too many *X-Files* episodes. All in preparation for this moment.

As the image on the video monitor comes into focus, gasps of shock and disbelief permeate the small room. Is it some hideous alien creature on the screen, some terrifying microscopic monster? No. The image on the screen is a grapelike cluster of cells, identical to those of *Staphylococcus aureus,* a common terrestrial anaerobic bacterium. As eyes close and shoulders slump, the worst nightmare of the scientists is realized. A seven-year experiment with a slim but tantalizing possibility of answering the age-old question of life on Mars may be invalidated. All because terrestrial bacteria must have hitched a ride into space on the very instruments used to drill into the Martian rocks. But then again, what if a single genesis produced life on Mars and Earth and the bacteria are actually hardy Martian cousins?

This fictional scenario is a real-life worry for scientists currently working on missions to collect rock samples from Mars and bring them safely back to Earth. Contamination of drill bits with Earthly microbes is more than a remote possibility. It is sufficiently difficult to build and launch ships into orbit without the added problems associated with having to work under completely sterile conditions. Faced with the possibility that sterility cannot be assured, how will it be possible to determine what is alien and what is not?

If alien life is found in our solar system, first contact will likely be with simple cells rather then either little green men or the "grays" so ubiquitous in accounts of alien abduction. Since cells are the centerpiece of life on Earth, it is difficult to imagine an alien life-form that is not based on cells. Living on earth, however, does give us a bad case of biological solipsism. Mix together carbon, nitrogen, oxygen, phosphorous, and plenty of water, wait a few billion years, and what could possibly emerge except cellular life?

All life on Earth is composed of cells. English scientist Robert Hooke used a primitive microscope to observe cells in plant material in the mid-seventeenth century, but his observations remained unappreciated for 170 years until the German naturalist Theodor Schwann correctly theorized that all organisms consisted of cells. The next major advance came in 1858, when German physician Rudolf Virchow suggested that all cells come from other cells. This was a remarkable statement in its day, that life springs from life and not non-life. The problem, of course, was getting people to believe him, for who had not seen mold appear on bread where no mold was before? Soon after Virchow's hypothesis was publicized, French microbiologist Louis Pasteur proved to skeptical scientists that life did indeed spring from preexisting life. Modern biology still considers the cell as the basic unit of life.

Cells existed for at least 3.85 billion years before being discovered by Robert Hooke. Rocks of this age from Western Greenland contain tiny bits of chemicals that are thought to be the remnants of early cellular life. Actual fossilized cells are visible in rocks dating back a mere 3.5 billion years from Australia and South Africa. Since the Earth was formed about 4.5 billion years ago, cellular life took 750 million years to develop from the original simmering primordial soup. These ancient cells needed to be especially sturdy, given the turbulent times on early Earth. It is hard to imagine trying to make a home and getting to the important business of evolving given the exploding volcanoes and constant meteor showers. Some of the meteorite impacts were so violent, they vaporized the upper layer of oceans. These turbulent times ended about 3.85 billion years ago, giving our hardy little ancestors a chance to spread throughout the planet. In short, cellular life pretty much formed almost as soon as the planet settled down enough to permit it.

Modern cells come in so many shapes and sizes that it is impossible to predict what an alien cell might look like. Some cells are very large: a chicken egg is a single cell; some human nerve cells can stretch over three feet, from the base of the spinal cord down to the toes. Some cells are extremely small, such as bacteria, and can be seen only with the help of powerful microscopes. But all cells, no matter what the shape or size, are a liquid compartment surrounded by a barrier called a plasma membrane, which is composed of lipids (the same molecules in fats) and proteins. The membrane separates molecules inside the cell from the environment. It must be strong enough to keep out large predators like viruses yet sufficiently permeable to let in food and water and flush out wastes. Formation of a plasma membrane was the key to the origin of life.

All life is a series of chemical reactions, in which molecules must physically come together so that new molecules can be formed. Molecules trapped in a compartment by the plasma membrane are confined to a small space, making it much more likely that they will interact with one another. Imagine how long it would take to build a house if the building materials are scattered randomly all over the city. Now consider building the same house if all the materials lie within a fence that surrounds the property. Although alien membranes might have different types of lipids and proteins, it is hard to imagine life-forms developing in their absence.

Television aliens are rarely cells unless they are some giant space-faring amoebae sucking up the starship *Enterprise*. Some TV aliens look like giant copies of animals that already exist on Earth. Other aliens look like humans with bad makeup—after all, costumes have to fit the actors wearing them. Screen aliens do things that give away the fact that they're not your average Tom, Dick, or Harry, like emerging from spaceships on the Washington, D.C., mall with giant robot companions named "Klaatu." While some of the aliens on *The X-Files* are just as fanciful, such as the morphing, green-blooded bounty hunter from the episode "Herrenvolk," others are much more subtle, and therefore more plausible. There are alien worms buried near a meteorite in the episode "Ice," and strange microbes in flasks labeled "Purity Control" in the episode "The Erlenmeyer Flask"; the aliens in the episodes "Gethsemane" and "Redux" are not necessarily the ones that resemble refugees from Roswell, New Mexico, but rather unclassifiable cells that begin to divide when placed in a nutrient media; and finally, there is the so-called black cancer organism introduced in the episode "Piper Maru," which changes from dust into sluglike worms that invade helpless human hosts.

On *The X-Files*, differentiation between what is alien and what is merely strange falls within the auspices of Scully and the numerous scientific experts with whom she consults. These researchers use the latest techniques to ferret out the truth of the organisms entrusted to them. It's a dangerous business. Scientists who analyze alien life-forms on *The X-Files* have much in common with red-shirted security men from the original *Star Trek* series—they rarely survive the episode. You would think that after six seasons and so many deaths, scientists would run screaming from the room at first sight of either Mulder or Scully. Yet without these brave and dedicated individuals, the truth would remain hidden.

Although real scientists have not yet faced the question of living aliens, speculation has fueled commentaries for years on such subjects as whether alien bacteria are sailing the heavens on comets or dust, and whether life originated elsewhere and we are all aliens to this planet. Like many of my scientist friends, I love to fantasize about what alien life-forms might be like. As a biochemist, I think more about the insides of alien organisms than the outsides. What would the genetic material look like? Will the proteins be similar? Will similar plasma membranes enclose the cells? Helping to add realism to the scientific investigations of alien organisms on *The X-Files* has been wonderful because I can make some of my own personal speculations come to life.

How to Identify an Alien in Three Easy Steps

INT. GEORGETOWN MICROBIOLOGY DEPT.—LUNCH ROOM—LATE NIGHT

DR. CARPENTER

What you're looking at is a sequence of genes from the bacteria you brought in. Normally, we'd see no gaps in the sequence. But with these bacteria, we do.

SCULLY

Why is that?

Dr. Carpenter takes a deep breath, staring at Scully for a long beat.

                     DR. CARPENTER

I don't know why, but I'll tell you that my first call would, under any other circumstances, have been to the government.

                     SCULLY

What exactly did you find?

                     DR. CARPENTER

A fifth and sixth DNA nucleotide. A new base pair.
               (beat)
What you are looking at, Agent Scully, exists nowhere in nature. It would have to be, by definition, extraterrestrial.

                           —"The Erlenmeyer Flask"

The *X-Files* episode "The Erlenmeyer Flask" begins with a high-speed police chase. The fugitive, however, is anything but routine. When cornered by the police, he moves with lightning speed and strikes with a strength well beyond that of a normal man. These attributes by themselves are sufficient to pique the curiosity of Mulder. Add green blood and the ability to breathe under water and even Scully can't help but be intrigued.

When Mulder and Scully visit the laboratory of Dr. Berubi, Harvard Medical School class of '64 and the owner of the fugitive's car, they find him busy doing experiments with microbes and monkeys. Like any practitioner of the arts of molecular biology, Dr. Berubi's lab is decorated with numerous Erlenmeyer flasks. Whether glass or more modern plastic, these conical-shaped containers designed by German chemist Richard Erlenmeyer have been used for over one hundred years to grow microorganisms.

While Mulder and Scully are questioning Dr. Berubi, they become curious about the microbes being grown in Erlenmeyer flasks labeled "Purity Control." Did these microscopic entities contribute to the transformation of the good doctor's colleague from hardworking scientist into authority-evading, water-breathing, green-blooded strongman? Since Dr. Berubi is decidedly uncooperative, Mulder and

Scully leave but return later to discover that the doctor has swan-dived from an upper floor window using laboratory gauze around his neck instead of the more traditional rubber ropes around the ankles. The suspicious death of Dr. Berubi has increased Mulder's curiosity. What is a dead genetics expert like Dr. Berubi growing in those Er-lenmeyer flasks? And what experiments require so many angry monkeys? Mulder hands a flask of microbes to Scully and asks her to investigate.

The scientific investigation of the cells growing in the Erlen-meyer flask plays a significant role in this episode. Chris Carter, while writing the script, wanted the experiments to be as accurate as possi-ble. Thus began several long conversations between Chris and myself to map out how a scientist would analyze an unknown microbe. Al-though my expertise is viruses rather then bacteria, I was well aware of the standard series of experiments that scientists perform when faced with an unidentified microorganism. I told Chris that the first step is to grow more of the sample using Erlenmeyer flasks and a nu-tritive liquid the color of weak coffee. Chris was apparently delighted by the name of the flask as this was to become the title of the episode. The second step, I told him, is to examine the appearance of the mi-crobes using the proper microscopes. Once you know what the cells look like, the third step is to analyze their DNA so the microbes can be classified with respect to known organisms.

Tempting some bacteria to grow and divide in the laboratory has been an endless nightmare for many microbiologists. The litany of excuses for why so many bacteria resist enticements to reproduce has been repeated by many scientists: they might be dead—but this can't be true for all recalcitrant bacteria—or they might not be partial to the cuisine. In general, the richer the food fed to difficult bacteria, the sicker they become; starving seems like a natural state for many microbes. The problem scientists face when trying to grow many mi-croorganisms is that some microbes need almost nothing of every-thing—just a few special, nearly impossible to discover ingredients, without which the bacteria refuse to cooperate and multiply.

Since portraying the endless trials and errors of trying to find a proper food source for bacteria would have TV viewers yawning as they frantically reach for the remote control, Dr. Berubi has already solved the mystery of growing the organism. Scully therefore proceeds to the second step, determining what the bacteria look like. She takes the flask of microbes to scientist Dr. Anne Carpenter at Georgetown University for enlightenment.

Invariably, investigations of any unknown microbe require microscopes. But which microscopes? There are so many to choose from. More often than not, the wrong type is used by television scientists. It is the misuse of microscopes, which always makes me wince, that made me so pleased when Chris first called for advice. At long last, a show existed that will use the correct microscopes because the person in charge cares about accuracy.

Take the light microscope, for example. Available as children's toys and routinely used by millions of high school students, these microscopes magnify specimens illuminated by light. The earliest light microscopes were simply upside-down telescopes. The Italian astronomer Galileo, when not examining the heavens, turned his telescope over and was amazed to see tiny bugs expand to the size of locusts. The earliest microscopes contained merely a single lens and were not much better than magnifying glasses. In the late-sixteenth century, the compound microscope was invented. By using more than one lens in combination, it provided dramatically improved resolution and a new world became visible overnight. Intricate details of fleas, gnats, hairs, nettle leaves, and razor edges were marveled over by naturalists using microscopes of cardboard and wood covered with vellum or ray skin.

In 1665, Robert Hooke, perhaps the most accomplished experimental scientist of the seventeenth century,[1] published *Micrographia*, in which he described his observations of the structure of a piece of cork and saw honeycomb divisions that looked like "a great many little boxes . . . the first *microscopical* pores I ever saw, and, perhaps, that were ever seen." Hooke named the tiny compartments "cellulae," the Latin name for "small rooms." The world of cells was born. Later in the seventeenth century, the Dutch amateur scientist (but highly skilled lens grinder) Antonie von Leeuwenhoek made the first obser-

---

[1]Hooke's extraordinary list of accomplishments includes the invention of the respirator, the universal joint, the anemometer, and barometer; authorship of the theory of combustion; contributions to physics, astronomy, mathematics, architecture, and, of course, biology.

vations of single-celled organisms like bacteria, opening up an entire new world of creatures never before imagined.

Light microscopes have undergone a number of improvements over the years. The current resolving power of a light microscope is about 200 nanometers (about one hundred thousandth of an inch), roughly four hundred times better than the human eye. The light that is used to illuminate specimens provides the resolution limitations of these microscopes. Light waves are subject to diffraction; the waves bend around obstacles in their way, causing the visible image to become less focused. What this means is that conventional light microscopes are powerful enough to see individual bacteria, but can't resolve defining features on their surfaces. Light microscopes can be used only to view the few giant viruses, despite what numerous television shows would like to suggest.

One of the most exciting recent developments in light microscopes is the confocal microscope. The confocal scope produces a greatly amplified image using a laser beam sent through a tiny pinhole. By scanning a specimen in the directions of height, width, and depth, a three-dimensional image is built up by powerful computers. I first told Chris about confocal scopes for the episode "Herrenvolk," in which Scully uses one to get a three-dimensional image of her smallpox vaccination scar.

Early in the twentieth century, German scientists saw an analogy between streams of electrons and waves of light. The radical idea was that a beam of electrons could be controlled and focused within a vacuum by magnets and work like the glass lenses of a microscope, only with much higher resolution. The first "electron microscope" was built in 1931. Over the following decades, improvements in design turned the electron microscope into one of biology's most important tools to examine the microscopic world.

There are two kinds of electron microscopes and both have been used in *X-Files* episodes. The first is called a transmission electron microscope. This microscope is used to view molecules like DNA or the interior of cells. The second type, a scanning electron microscope, is used only to see the outsides of objects, like the mutant flies in the episode "The Post-Modern Prometheus" and the alien bacteria in "The Erlenmeyer Flask." Scanning electron microscopes have produced some of the most breathtaking three-dimensional portraits of the very small and brought great insight to the ultrastructure of everything from cells to hair.

The main disadvantage of electron microscopy is that the specimen must be dead. It can provide amazing snapshots of life, but it can't be used to see life in action. Recently, refinements have been made to confocal microscopes such that they now can give electron microscope resolution of live specimens. If any living alien microscopic organisms are ever recovered, this would be the microscope of choice, so that the precious live sample need not be wasted.

I told Chris that the proper microscope to use for an up close and personal view of Berubi's microbes would be a scanning electron microscope. Dr. Carpenter and Scully marvel at the image of the strange cells on the scope's video monitor. When talking with Scully, Dr. Carpenter refers to the microbes as bacteria. Bacteria and similar-looking microbes called Archaea are collectively known as prokaryotes. Prokaryotes are considered by most scientists to be the ancestral cells—the oldest, simplest, and most primitive life-forms on Earth. Prokaryotes are merely a single cell, one compartment surrounded by the plasma membrane barrier. Floating around in the liquid or cytoplasm of the compartment are all the molecules required for life—the DNA genome or genetic material, along with proteins, sugars, lipids, minerals, and many others. The absence of smaller compartments inside a prokaryotic cell is their defining characteristic and what differentiates prokaryotes from cells of higher organisms, known as eukaryotes. When Dr. Carpenter describes the strange cells as bacteria, she must believe that they do not sequester their DNA genomes in a separate cubicle called a nucleus as do eukaryotic cells. Failure to separate the DNA from the rest of the cell is the hallmark of a prokaryote.

In my conversation with Chris, we discussed what Dr. Berubi's bacteria should look like. Scientists that specialize in the study of bacteria find their tiny research subjects to be fascinating and picturesque. I, on the other hand, can be more objective since I prefer plants and viruses to bacteria. While bacteria are fascinating, their appearance is prosaic at best. Since the bacteria in the episode were supposed to be alien, I suggested to Chris that he use a picture of something much more interesting, like plant pollen grains (my working with plants has nothing to do with finding them to be fascinating and picturesque). Pollen grains make wonderful alien bacteria. They are symmetrical like bacteria yet have intricate, complex surfaces with multiple pits and protrusions. I was delighted with the electron microscope picture of pollen that Chris used in the episode. The grains looked eerily alien as the camera focused in on their ornate pits. After the episode aired, Chris and I chuckled over his reading on a fledgling *X-Files* web site that several observant fans noticed that the alien "bacteria" looked suspiciously like pollen.

Since the "bacteria" that Scully and Dr. Carpenter see on the video monitor of the scanning electron microscope do not resemble normal bacteria, Dr. Carpenter tells Scully that she wants to do further studies. My suggestion to Chris was that a scientist would next look inside a cell, since scanning electron microscopy only gives a view of a cell's surface. To begin visually dissecting a cell, Dr. Carpenter could perform a technique called freeze fracturing. After placing the bacteria in a preservative solution, she would flash freeze them in liquid nitrogen. By striking a frozen block containing the cells with a knife, cracks are created that pass through embedded cells. After Dr. Carpenter sprays the cracked surfaces with platinum, the metal cast is removed and an impression of cells in the metal is viewed with a scanning electron microscope. Dr. Carpenter would see an exquisitely detailed, three-dimensional view of the beautifully ordered plasma membrane that separates a bacterium's single cellular compartment from the outside environment. If the strange microbes were like all cells on Earth, she would see that the plasma membrane is composed of two rows of lipids that completely cover the cell. The perfect symmetry of the lipid rows would be broken by scattered proteins that transverse the membrane.

Besides freeze fracturing Dr. Berubi's bacteria to examine their membranes, Dr. Carpenter would have sliced the cells into many thin wafers using a diamond knife. After staining these ultrathin cell sections with lead, she would use a transmission electron microscope to see exquisite details of the interior of the cell. Scully phones Mulder to report that she and Dr. Carpenter have found something astonishing inside the bacteria—tiny cells that resemble chloroplasts. Scully tells Mulder that bacteria such as these haven't existed for countless years. What Scully is describing are bacteria that may have lived more than 1.5 billion years ago—bacteria in the process of evolving into eukaryotic cells.

Eukaryotes such as protists (amoebas), animals, and plants have within their cells a number of small cubicles in addition to the nucleus that houses the DNA. These cubicles are called organelles and each is surrounded by a membrane. Some of the little cubicles resemble intact prokaryotic cells, complete with their own little DNA genomes. This observation caused biologist Lynn Margulis to propose that billions of years ago, a large, hungry prokaryote gobbled up one of its harmless little prokaryotic neighbors and forgot to digest it. The tiny prokaryote (no doubt breathing a sigh of relief) continued to live inside the larger cell. Eventually, the two cells came to agreeable terms and developed a symbiotic relationship, with both cells contributing to the well-being of the new entity. The ingested prokaryote lost the ability to ever live a separate life and became an integral part of the larger cell. Together, the new entity developed into the earliest eukaryotic cell. Mitochondria, found in all eukaryotic cells, and chloroplasts, which reside exclusively in plant cells, are descendants of such poorly digested prokaryotic snacks. What Scully believes she has discovered is that Dr. Berubi's bacteria are in an early stage of symbiosis with the progenitors of chloroplasts. She is correct when saying that such bacteria have not existed on Earth for over a billion years.

Dr. Carpenter conducts a third experiment while Scully sleeps in a nearby room. She analyzes some of the organism's DNA. One of the inescapable features of cells on our planet is that DNA is the genetic material, also called the genome, of the cell. If Dr. Berubi's strange-looking bacteria have a genome consisting of standard DNA, then the DNA would be composed of the same four constituents, called nucleotides, that are found in the DNA of all earthly organisms. Just as a protein is a chain of amino acids linked one after another, DNA is a chain of nucleotides. The smallest chains of DNA are the genomes of viruses, some of which are only a few thousand nucleotides long. A DNA chain in humans can be hundreds of millions of nucleotides long.

DNA rarely exists as a single chain. Rather, nearly all DNA is composed of two chains of nucleotides that coil around each other to form the famous "double helix." The two chains of the double helix are held together because nucleotides in one chain pair up and form weak chemical bonds, called hydrogen bonds, with nucleotides in the sister chain. The four nucleotides in DNA, abbreviated A, G, C, and T, always choose the same partners to pair with. The nucleotide A in one chain always pairs with T in the sister chain. Likewise, C always pairs with G. So if a short region of DNA in one chain is AATC, the sister chain would have the sequence TTAG. This means that if you know the order of nucleotides in one chain of a DNA molecule, you automatically know the nucleotide order in its sister chain.

Since DNA has only four different constituents, scientists in the first half of the twentieth century thought that it couldn't possibly contain enough information to be a cell's genetic material. After all, the genetic material, the genome of the organism, must contain the entire program for producing a unique living creature. The structure of DNA also seemed too simple—merely a uniform double helix regardless of whether the DNA came from bacteria or humans. It seemed much more reasonable that proteins with their twenty different amino acid constituents and their infinite variety of sizes and shapes were the cell's genetic program. Yet a computer program at its most basic level is a language of only two constituents, zeros and ones. The complexity behind programs as intricate as Windows 98 is achieved by the precise order of billions of these two numbers. The complexity of DNA was likewise found to be a function of the order of nucleotides and not the simple number of different constituents

Dr. Carpenter explains to Scully that she has sequenced (determined the order of nucleotides in) one of the organism's genes. If the DNA in a cell is analogous to a computer's hard drive, then genes can be thought of as programs on the hard drive. Genes are the basic unit of heredity. They are the genetic programs that determine everything from the color of your hair to how shy you are around other people. Genes are regions of DNA that get copied into DNA's molecular cousin, RNA. RNA is similar to DNA in that it is also a chain of linked nucleotides, but the nucleotides used to construct RNA are slightly different than the nucleotides that make up DNA. Most RNA molecules are the instruction sheets given to cellular machines called ribosomes, which in turn use the information to construct proteins. The order of nucleotides in thousands of different DNA genes is therefore what determines the order of nucleotides in the corresponding RNA instruction sheets, which get translated by the thousands of ribosomes in a cell into proteins with a particular order of amino acids.

Although proteins are not the genetic material of the cell, they are what directly determines your appearance and basic behavioral traits.

The particular gene that Dr. Carpenter would have sequenced is the one called ribosomal DNA. This gene specifies the production of an RNA molecule called ribosomal RNA. Ribosomal RNA, unlike most RNAs, is not an instruction sheet for making proteins. Rather, ribosomal RNA is one of the numerous cellular ingredients that together make up a ribosome. Since all cells need to make proteins, all cells contain ribosomes. When a new creature is discovered, whether it be a simple bacterium or complex animal, scientists examine the order of nucleotides in its ribosomal DNA gene. Once determined, the sequence is compared with ribosomal DNA sequences of other known organisms. Organisms that are more closely related have genes that share more similar orders of nucleotides. By comparing the ribosomal DNA sequences for all known organisms, a "tree of life" can be drawn, with the earliest organisms at the base, and the most recently emerging organisms forming the outermost branches. If species are near each other on the tree, this means that their DNA sequences are closely related.

An organism unrelated to life on our planet might have a cellular biochemistry that is beyond our imagination. Such a creature would probably not have DNA as we know it, let alone have ribosomal DNA genes. If Dr. Carpenter determines that her strange organism contains ribosomal DNA genes and that the nucleotide sequences of these genes are similar to those found in other organisms on Earth, she would conclude that it was simply a strange new type of bacterium. But this is *The X-Files*, so that isn't what she finds.

When Chris originally talked with me about this script, he needed Dr. Carpenter to discover something about the bacteria that would instantly suggest an extraterrestrial origin. My suggestion was for Dr. Carpenter to discover something completely unexpected when she is sequencing some of the organism's DNA. She would find that Dr. Berubi's bacteria contain DNA with six nucleotides instead of the usual four.

So how could Dr. Carpenter make this startling finding? DNA sequencing is now a routine laboratory procedure. The results of such an experiment are displayed as four ladders, one for each of the four DNA nucleotides, on a piece of X-ray film called a sequencing autoradiograph. With a few minutes of simple instruction, even a child can look at the finished film and determine the order of nucleotides in a sequenced DNA fragment. Although *The X-Files'* audience was unlikely to have a detailed grasp of modern molecular biology, I suggested to Chris that Dr. Carpenter find gaps in the nucleotide ladders on the X-ray film of the organism's DNA sequence. These gaps could be interpreted as evidence of an additional pair of nucleotides—a fifth and sixth nucleotide not found in nature.

Dr. Carpenter explains to Scully (and the home audience) that DNA is always composed of two different pairs of nucleotides, the A/T pair and the C/G pair. Evidence for a third pair of nucleotides in DNA is so unexpected and so different from DNA in any life-form on Earth that she has to conclude the bacteria are extraterrestrial. Chris asked me what I would do if I came across such a result in my own work. I laughed and said that I would probably call the government (not that I ever envision making such a phone call). Dr. Carpenter tells Scully in the episode that normally, her first call would have been to the government. But government agent Dana Scully is already present to share the startling news of the existence of extraterrestrials.

Since no normal DNA-sequencing autoradiograph would contain gaps, I agonized over how such an autoradiograph could be artificially doctored for the episode. I soon realized that this was taking scientific accuracy to a ridiculous level. I suggested to Chris that he visit a molecular biology lab at the University of British Columbia, near where *The X-Files* is filmed, and ask for a standard "sequencing autoradiograph," which I dutifully spelled out. I suggested that Chris have Dr. Carpenter point to the nucleotide-sequence ladders on the X-ray film and exclaim to Scully that she has found gaps in the sequence. This no doubt disappointed the 0.00001 percent of the population who could interpret the real autoradiograph shown in the episode and clearly see that there are no gaps in the DNA sequence.

Dr. Carpenter and Scully find one more intriguing property of the alien bacteria: they are filled with virus. Since thousands of viruses can be present in an infected cell, it is usually a simple matter to recognize if cells are experiencing a virus invasion by using a transmission electron microscope. Viruses can infect nearly all types of cells—bacterial, fungal, plant or animal—so it is not surprising that alien bacteria also contain virus. Although it is a rare cell that doesn't need to worry about virus infection, a single virus is adapted to infect organisms only from one of life's six taxonomic kingdoms. Viruses that infect bacteria cannot infect members of the Archaea (the other type of prokaryote), protists (such as amoebas), fungi, plants, or animals, and vice versa. However, viruses can infect several different hosts within a kingdom. Influenza virus, which causes most cases of the flu, can infect birds, pigs, and humans. The virus that I study, my much-beloved turnip crinkle virus, can infect turnips, mustard, Chinese cabbage, and a lovely little weed called *Arabidopsis thaliana*. Despite viruses' varied appearances and hosts, they all have a single-minded goal: invade a cell, hijack its ribosomes, and force the cell to produce more virus as quickly as possible.

Viruses are simply a set of genes on the prowl. The most rudimentary viruses are merely a protein bag stuffed with one or more pieces of DNA or RNA. Viruses have no independent metabolism. They cannot make proteins or copy their genome, so they must find a cell that is able, if not willing, to help. Relating back to our previous analogy, if the DNA genome of a cell is like a computer's hard drive, then a virus is a bag containing a program on a floppy disk. If there is no way to open the bag, or no computer to insert the disk into, the program is without meaning. Viruses are not cells. The average size of a virus is only about one hundredth the size of a cell. Viruses have no nucleus, no ribosomes, no metabolic activity. They can't absorb nutrients or make proteins. If a virus cannot find a cell to infect, it has no existence.

Since I work on viruses, students often ask me if viruses are alive. I like to answer this question with the question, "How do you define life?"[2] Since this generally leads to vacant stares, I usually issue the reassuring statement that entire books have been written trying to explain the scientific meaning of life.

Most scientists will agree that cells are the basic unit of life, but why? At the very least, something that is alive should have a metabolism, the ability to either absorb or create the materials required for its existence. It should be able to reproduce itself, and evolve into

[2]Occasionally this prompts the follow-up, "Why do you always answer a question with a question?" To this, my standard response is, "Do I?"

forms better suited to its environment. The simplest organisms that fulfill these parameters are cells. But as a fan of science fiction, I would argue that the future will likely see a change in this definition. With computer and robot designs becoming increasingly sophisticated, the future could see the emergence of sentient machines with control centers that mimic the human brain. Although no one will argue that an automobile is alive, who will argue that an intelligent and self-aware machine is not as alive as a bacterium?

To invade an animal cell, a virus must trick the cell into letting it through the membrane. Getting most large substances through the plasma membrane barrier and into a cell requires the help of receptors, the puzzle piece–like proteins that sit on the surfaces of cells and serve as gatekeepers, allowing in only those substances that the cell needs. When a specific molecule passes by that can fit together with a receptor, a doorway into the cell is activated. Viruses have cleverly exploited this doorway by having proteins or sugars on their surfaces that mimic the shape of natural molecules in the body which normally interact with receptors. When a virus binds to a receptor, the receptor doesn't realize that it's being duped and opens a way for the virus to invade the cell. Since different cells have different sets of receptors, viruses are limited to infecting only the cells that have a receptor with which they can interact. This is why viruses like the human immunodeficiency virus (HIV) can only infect certain types of cells like immune-system cells and various brain cells—cells that have the virus's receptor, called CD4, on their surfaces.

As the virus sneaks into a cell, the protein bag is opened and the genome of the virus is released. If the virus has a DNA genome, the viral DNA enters the nucleus and commandeers the cell's enzymes to make RNA copies of its genes. The virus subtly alters the cell's ribosomes, causing them to ignore the cell's own RNA and translate only the virus's RNA into proteins. If the viral genome is RNA instead of DNA, the task is even simpler. The viral RNA is directly used to make proteins. Some of the new proteins are enzymes that replicate the genome of the virus. Other proteins are made that form the virus's coat, the bag that surrounds the viral genome. When all is ready, newly made protein bags assemble around freshly made virus genomes. Most animal and bacterial viruses then burst through the superfluous and fatally injured cell and hunt for more virgin cells to infect.

So what was Dr. Berubi doing with an Erlenmeyer flask filled with alien bacteria replete with viruses and chloroplasts? Scully and Mulder speculate that Dr. Berubi was using the bacteria to grow virus and then using the virus to transfer genes into monkeys and his assistant. Using viruses to transfer genes between organisms, even between kingdoms, is not science fiction.[3] Some viruses with DNA genomes can insert their DNA into the genome of the infected host. It is not a difficult matter to splice a foreign piece of DNA into the virus's DNA (for professionals, at least; don't try it at home). Then, when the virus naturally inserts its genome into the DNA of the host, the new piece of DNA is inserted as well. Dr. Berubi was using bacteria as many scientists do, as a convenient means of producing additional copies of the genome of his engineered virus. To successfully amplify a virus genome in bacteria, the virus first must be disguised as an ordinary piece of bacterial DNA. To accomplish this deception, scientists adds bits of bacterial DNA to the virus DNA. One of these DNA bits contains a bacterial origin of replication. In this way, the bacteria's enzymes think that they are replicating the bacteria's DNA when they are really replicating the virus's DNA. Mulder and Scully's idea that Berubi is using the bacteria as a living factory to grow virus is thus a distinct possibility.

Another piece of the puzzle comes from Dr. Berubi's file folder. Dr. Berubi was working on the Human Genome Project, which Mulder calls the largest scientific project ever undertaken in the history of science. Mulder's description of the Human Genome Project is accurate. It is an immense, multibillion-dollar, fifteen-year effort to determine the precise order of the 6 billion nucleotides of the human genome. It is the twentieth-century equivalent to ordering the one hundred known elements of the periodic table, except that the ordering involves 100,000 human genes.

Dr. Berubi is not alone in working on the Human Genome Project. This monumental effort involves over 250 laboratories in the United States along with labs in eighteen other countries. When you consider that the largest genome sequenced to date is that of the common baker's yeast, a seven-year effort involving a mere 12 million nucleotides and six thousand genes, the Human Genome Project seems overwhelming. But by starting with smaller genomes, such as

---

[3]For a more complete explanation, you'll have to wait for Chapter 4.

those of bacteria and yeast, technology has led to more efficient automation of DNA sequencing. Although less than 3 percent of the human genome has been finished so far, scientists believe that they will comfortably make their 2005 goal.

Once the genome is sequenced, scientists and medical doctors will quickly be able to identify genes involved in genetic diseases like some forms of cancer. Individuals that are predisposed to particular diseases will also be identified and treatments will shift to prevention-based approaches. As is revealed in subsequent *X-Files* episodes, the goal of Dr. Berubi and secret forces in the government is to use viruses to insert alien DNA into humans and create alien-human hybrids. Dr. Berubi may have found that only certain individuals are able to survive the introduction of alien DNA. Through his work on the genome project, he could identify which genes give individuals the ability to survive and thus be able to predict who will benefit from the alien DNA and who will die.

While Scully and Dr. Carpenter are working on the strange contents of the Erlenmeyer flask, Dr. Berubi's green-blooded assistant and recipient of the alien DNA is found and carted off to a hospital in an ambulance. While en route the paramedics, fearing their patient is dying, attempt to do a needle decompression procedure. When the needle penetrates the skin, toxic fumes come from the body causing the paramedics to faint.

This scene was written not long after a similar incident became a major news story. In 1994, thirty-one-year-old Gloria Ramirez, now known on the Internet as the "Toxic Lady," was rushed to the emergency room of Riverside General Hospital in California suffering from respiratory and cardiac distress related to her cervical cancer. While drawing blood, a nurse noticed a strange, ammonialike odor and fainted. A doctor took a whiff of the syringe with the patient's blood and also passed out. By the time the incident was over, four additional ER workers had fainted and twenty-eight other people were affected. Gloria Ramirez died in the ER of kidney failure a short time later.

The scene at the hospital must have resembled an *X-Files* episode. The ER was evacuated. Riverside city HAZ MAT (Hazardous Materials) teams dressed in space suit–like apparel took air samples, decontaminated the room, and sealed Gloria's body. If this were a fictitious incident in an *X-Files* episode, Mulder and Scully would have arrived soon afterward. Scully would have conducted the autopsy, finding some scientific basis for the white flecks in Gloria's blood. Mulder would have questioned family members about whether Ms. Ramirez complained of being an alien abductee or whether she recently visited sites of illegal pesticide sprayings. The case would be solved and the X-File closed.

Life, however, rarely imitates fiction. The autopsy of Ms. Ramirez was inconclusive. White particles in her blood could not be explained. There were no traces of ingested pesticides, which have occasionally produced odors in ERs. The hospital was ruled out as a source of the toxic fumes. Mass hysteria or previously undiagnosed medical conditions of the ER personnel were deemed highly unlikely. Dr. Julie Gorchynski, one of the first affected, had been a champion surfer in glowing health. Muscle spasms and oxygen loss following the incident have led to a rare destructive bone disorder. This real X-File remains open and unsolved.

Scully returns to finish helping Dr. Carpenter analyze the alien microbes, only to learn that Dr. Carpenter and her entire family were killed in a car crash. The death of Dr. Carpenter affected me in a rather unusual way. You see, Dr. Carpenter was named after me. Chris had told me that he would name the scientist in the episode Dr. Anne Simon. It was pure bad luck that another Anne Simon was a scientist at Georgetown University, where the fictitious Dr. Carpenter worked. The name therefore needed to be changed to my first name and my husband's last name. Before reading the script, I had visions of Dr. Anne Carpenter as a recurring character providing insightful scientific analysis season after season. My only hope now is that Dr. Carpenter faked her own death and is hiding somewhere, waiting for the opportunity to rise again and help Mulder and Scully in their quest for the truth.

Alien Hitchhikers

INT. U.S. CUSTOMS PRIVATE SEARCH ROOM—NIGHT

CUSTOMS OFFICER
Would you mind telling me the kind of diplomatic work you do, sir? And what material you're transporting in these?

He lifts TWO METAL CYLINDRICAL CANISTERS into view.
ANGLE TO INCLUDE MAN
Reacting to the site of the canisters.

                        MAN
    That is—those are filled with biohazardous material.

                CUSTOMS OFFICER
    Then where is the paperwork? And why aren't the containers
    marked?

                        MAN
    Don't open those. Whatever you do. That material cannot be
    exposed.

                                        —"Tunguska"

At the end of long overseas trips, it seems foreordained that my luggage is searched by United States customs agents. The drill is so routine. A stony-faced man scatters my personal belongings all over the counter. Then eyes gleam and a smile tickles his lips when hearing that I am a scientist who works on plant viruses. The inevitable questions begin. "How many farms teeming with diseased crops have you visited, Dr. Simon?" "What insidious viruses are you bringing back into the country, Dr. Simon?" As the minutes tick by and my chances of making that connecting flight go from dim to nonexistent, it's easy to forget where customs agents belong on the tree of life. Still, on these agents' shoulders rests an important responsibility—protecting the United States from invasion of deadly foreign pathogens, illegal drugs, and Cuban cigars.

While these are not items that I generally carry in my luggage, a passenger in the X-Files' episode "Tunguska" is not so innocent. Despite pleas of diplomatic immunity, agents open his suitcase to find several suspicious-looking glass tubes containing a biohazardous substance. While this revelation should have provoked some care in handling the containers, one slips out of an agent's clumsy fingers and shatters on the hard floor. Within seconds, a black, oily powder congeals into tiny, sluglike worms. The agent gasps in horror as the creatures slither under his pants legs and invade his body.

Unaware of this event, Mulder and Scully receive a tip that they should intercept a rock that is carried by another courier. The black, stony nature of the rock indicates that it is a meteorite. At the Department of Exobiology, Goddard Space Center, Dr. Sacks examines the rock and makes a startling discovery. He tells Mulder and Scully that the rock is indeed a meteorite and one that contains polycyclic aromatic hydrocarbons.

Polycyclic aromatic hydrocarbons, or PAHs, are a set of organic molecules composed of carbons and hydrogens arranged in a ring-shaped pattern. Take a breath in a heavily polluted urban area and your body will have an intimate association with PAHs. The major source of PAHs in the atmosphere is poorly combusted fossil fuels provided by autos and industrial plant emissions. Even minute doses of PAHs can cause cancer. Ever heard the advice against eating too much charcoal-broiled meat? That's because PAHs are released from charcoal, especially mesquite, and absorbed into the grilled food. Vegetables can also take up PAHs from the atmosphere while they are growing, especially large and leafy ones like lettuce and tobacco.

The PAHs that Dr. Sacks finds are in the interior of the mysterious rock, so they did not arise from the meteorite slamming into a barbecue alongside a Los Angeles freeway. Dr. Sacks is excited to find PAHs inside the meteorite because he knows that PAHs are produced by dead, decaying organisms. In other words, PAHs can be a sign that living creatures once resided inside the rock. Dr. Sacks determines that the PAHs in Mulder and Scully's rock are similar to those scientists found in the Antarctic meteorite ALH84001—the Martian meteorite with tantalizing but highly controversial signs of ancient life.

Of the twelve pieces of Mars that have been found on Earth, ALH84001 is by far the oldest—a potato-sized, 4.5-billion-year-old rock that weighs a little over four pounds (1.9 kg). Scientists can say with certainty that these meteorites were once part of the Martian landscape by analyzing gases trapped inside minute bubbles of glass within the rocks.[4] The glass found in ALH84001 is evidence that the

[4]While these meteorites were found as far back as 1865, only since the Viking mission have we known enough about the Martian atmosphere to know their origin.

rock was once near a cataclysmic event, a comet or asteroid smashing into Mars with such violence that small parts of ALH84001 melted and formed bubbles of glass. Trapped within the tiny bubbles are whiffs of the atmosphere of Mars, which the Viking mission of 1976 measured to be 95 percent carbon dioxide, 2.7 percent nitrogen, 1.6 percent argon, and a few trace gases.

If you think about it, the presence of Martian rocks on Earth is pretty remarkable. For an object to be ejected from the surface of Mars into space, a comet or asteroid would have had to strike the planet with enough force to throw that object outward at a speed of nearly 4 miles per second—five times the velocity of a rifle. The pieces of Mars so launched would then remain in the solar system (leaving would require a velocity of more than 350 miles per second) for millions of years until captured by the Earth's gravitational field. One of those pieces, ALH84001, wandered homeless through the solar system for 16 million years before plummeting into the Antarctic. Thirteen thousand years later it was picked up by someone, only to languish unappreciated for eight more years in a cabinet at the Johnson Space Center in Houston.

ALH84001 is not your garden-variety Mars meteorite. Unlike its eleven more youthful siblings, it contains PAHs, the first evidence that organic molecules exist on Mars. This finding came as quite a shock. Over twenty years ago, two Viking space probes conducted experiments that tested for traces of organic compounds on the surface of Mars. One test came back positive, the other negative. NASA, not wanting to confuse the public, decided to issue a confident report stating that Mars was a lifeless wasteland devoid of organic materials. But similar positive and negative results were obtained when the two tests were conducted on the surface of Antarctica. NASA chose not to release a further statement that no life existed on Earth.[5] The tests conducted on Earth were not sensitive enough to detect the vast amounts of frozen fungi, algae, bacteria, and diatoms now known to lie deep below the ice surrounding the South Pole. One can only speculate on what the same tests may have missed on Mars.

Besides containing organic PAHs, ALH84001 has many tiny globules of carbonate, a substance that can form when water saturated with

[5]Take note, paranoid conspiracy theorists/X-Files fans.

carbon dioxide permeates through rock. Associated with the carbonate globules in the meteorite are chains of magnetite beads—an iron-oxygen compound. Finding carbonate, magnetite, or PAHs by themselves would hardly promote much excitement outside the world of geologists and astrophysicists. But carbonates usually indicate the presence of water, the elixir of life; magnetite beads in precisely the same chain patterns are often found with fossils of Earth bacteria, and the PAHs were of the type produced by decaying microbes. Discovery of all three compounds together within a hundred thousandth of an inch of objects identical to putative terrestrial miniature bacteria, and the tantalizing conclusion reached by respected NASA and Stanford scientists is that life existed and may still exist on Mars.

When NASA held a news conference to announce that ALH84001 contained signs of life, the story was featured on television and newspapers around the world. At my university, microfossils and life on Mars became the major topic of hallway conversations. While some residents of Earth probably wondered what all the fuss was about, others pondered the mind-boggling scientific and religious implications. Life on other planets would mean that we are not alone, that conditions on Earth are not uniquely suited to the development of living organisms.

With all the hype that followed the announcement by NASA, would you be surprised to learn that this was not the first report of fossils in meteorites? In the 1960s, George Claus and Bart Nagy used a hot new instrument called an electron microscope to examine meteorites known as the Orgeuil chondrite and the Ivuna rock. They were shocked to find minuscule shapes that looked like fossils of bacteria. Fearing contamination after impact, Claus and Nagy looked deep into the rocks yet still found the same lifelike structures. Realizing the implication of such findings, Claus and Nagy published a cautious paper in the journal *Nature* suggesting that maybe, just maybe they had found signs of ancient extraterrestrial life.

Claus and Nagy's paper was received with a tidal wave of criticism and indifference. The samples must have been altered after impact; the fossils were artifacts of the examination procedure; or simply, the "microfossils" had to be the result of natural, inorganic processes in the rock, since they were much too small to be real cells. Life on other planets in our solar system was a topic for *Star Trek* fans, not serious scientists. Conditions were too harsh on other planets. Even the best possibility for life outside of Earth, Mars, was too cold and the only surface water was frozen. The moons of Jupiter were too distant from the sun and the presence of liquid water was also thought to be highly improbable.

So why are reports of fossils in meteors being taken seriously today? It has to do with the attention given to the question, Where does life exist on Earth? Actually, the question isn't where life exists but where *doesn't* life exist. There are abundant microbes in the freezing cold of the Antarctic ice. Beneath the burning desert sands are not only bacteria but specialized insects. Twenty-five miles up in the atmosphere float bacteria. At the bottom of the deepest ocean, where no sunlight penetrates, where the temperature hovers right around freezing, and organic nutrients should be too dilute to support anything, exotic zoos of life survive.

But what really led scientists to open their minds to the possibility of fossils in Martian rocks was the abundance of life below our own ground. Microbiologists had once thought that microbes only lived in mud close to the surface. Below the surface layer was solid rock, and what could survive within rock? Yes, there were signs of bacteria deeper below the surface, but the bacteria couldn't be grown in the laboratory, and what couldn't be grown had to be dead or not very interesting.

Then the U.S. Department of Energy decided to check the quality of water below one of its nuclear plants. Deep holes were drilled near the Savannah River in South Carolina. What was uncovered was a world teeming with life, as much life as on the surface, maybe more. Miles beneath the ground, in what has been called the deep, dark biosphere, live bacteria and fungi, basking in the heat of the Earth's core and snacking on rocks and leftover organic material from dead neighbors. The bacteria even make their own organic molecules like methane—not by photosynthesis, which requires sunlight, but from carbon dioxide and hydrogen gas dissolved in the rock. Some scientists even believe that life began under the planet's surface. The abundance of life below our ground has made many scientists reevaluate whether surface searches for extraterrestrial life are giving misleading results.

Dr. Sacks's excitement in finding that the meteorite contains PAHs is therefore understandable—he believes that this meteorite may also contain signs of ancient extraterrestrial life. But PAHs by themselves are only one piece of the puzzle. Dr. Sacks tells Mulder and Scully that he wants to search for microfossils in the rock's interior. Scully correctly reminds Dr. Sacks that many scientists doubt that ALH84001 contains any fossils of ancient Martian life.

There are several reasons why a growing number of scientists are skeptical about fossils in ALH84001. To examine the meteorite, NASA scientists used the type of electron microscope that requires coating the subject with metal. Some geologists who specialize in the study of meteorites believe that the metal coating itself created the tiny objects that look like fossils. Other scientists believe that the fossils are just irregularities in the surface of minerals embedded in the rock. To counter these arguments, a French group recently used an advanced microscope called an environmental scanning electron microscope to examine a Tunisian meteorite called Tatahouine. Unlike conventional electron microscopes, this new device does not require coating the sample with metal. Looking at the Tatahouine meteorite in its natural form, they found objects that looked identical to the fossils in ALH84001. The Murchison meteorite from Australia also contains mushroom-shaped bodies that look like microfossils.

One of the arguments used to bolster the claims for Martian life is the striking resemblance of the tiny fossils to mysterious dwarf bacteria known as nanobacteria. Robert Folk of the University of Texas believes that nanobacteria are not only a major constituent of rocks and sediments buried deep below the surface of our planet, but are also found in tap water and tooth enamel. The size of nanobacteria, about one thousandth the volume of normal bacteria, is a cause of concern for many scientists. A cell this size is only big enough to contain a few ribosomes, a few hundred proteins, and only eight genes' worth of DNA. This is far, far less than what is necessary to support even the most primitive of bacteria.[6] For nanobacteria to be real cells, and not artifacts of the investigation methods, then they must have a biochemistry completely at odds with the biochemistry of all other organisms on Earth. While this may be a common occurrence in science fiction, it is much less likely to be true in real life.

[6]Scientists estimate that at least 250 genes are needed for a bacteria cell to survive and produce enough ingredients to allow it to replicate.

Other aspects of the report of ancient life in ALH84001 are also being questioned. Not every scientist believes that carbonates + magnetite + PAHs = life. At the heart of the controversy is the origin of the carbonate globules. Carbonates can form from water and carbon dioxide at low, life-compatible temperatures. It is crucial for the theory of life on Mars that there be evidence of liquid water. But carbonates can also form from liquid carbon dioxide as long as there is no water and a temperature of about 800 degrees Fahrenheit. Ralph Harvey of Case Western University and Harry McSween from the University of Tennessee believe that an asteroid crashed into Mars a billion years ago, liquefying the Martian surface and its covering of carbon dioxide frost, resulting in the carbonates found in ALH84001. According to Harvey and McSween, carbonates in the Martian rock do not imply the presence of water and life but just the opposite—searing heat in the absence of water, conditions where life could not possibly have existed.[7]

[7]If you aren't familiar with the scientific process, you might think that such diametrically opposed opinions when looking at the same piece of evidence have no place in the precise world of science. Ralph Harvey put the arguments over ALH84001 into perspective in the following piece that he wrote for the Internet:

> It is a completely normal part of science for researchers to "try on" various theories and interpretations, and at this stage utterly natural that groups might hold to contradictory interpretations. Normally the public doesn't see science at this stage, and I'm disappointed that they did in this case, because some might draw the conclusion that scientists are morons who can't make up their minds. In fact, that's the power of science—we take our time, examine all the possibilities, try hard to learn which data to trust and which data to mistrust. In the end, no theory answers all the questions, but usually a theory develops that successfully interprets the majority of the data, and offers predictions that are later seen to be fulfilled. Perhaps the most important aspect of science is that there's always some data somewhere that goes against the favored theory. Scientists don't ever discard those findings, because even though they are "sand in the gears," they often prove to be very important pieces of the puzzle in their own right, clues to phenomena we just didn't understand when we collected the data.

The tenor of this statement may seem familiar. It is what Scully faces week after week as she tries to make scientific sense out of events that can be beyond what science can easily explain.

Dr. Sacks is anxious to enter the debate on life in meteorites, so he prepares the meteorite for electron microscopy. Slicing through a section of the rock, Dr. Sacks must have instantly realized that an electron microscope would be superfluous. Oily black particles splatter onto the doctor, then congeal into slimy, sluglike worms. Before Dr. Sacks has time to be euphoric about discovering living organisms within the meteorite, the worms enter his body and he is paralyzed.

An organism that starts out as thousands of individual cells (like the black cancer particles) that then join together to form a single, multicellular creature sounds like a nightmare made for science fiction—but it isn't. *Dictyostelium discoideum* (known to fans as "dicti") is an organism called a cellular slime mold. Dicti goes through phases of its life where it resembles an ameoba, followed by an animal, then a plant, and finally a fungus. As an amoeba, single dicti cells are content to live a solitary existence, moving short distances and munching on bacteria for food. When an amoeba is hungry and bacteria are scarce, it releases a chemical that acts as a homing beacon to other dicti cells in the vicinity. The cells gather together and arrange themselves to form a single, multicellular slug. Dicti slugs bear an uncanny resemblance to the larger *X-Files* black cancer worms.

When the environment becomes dry, dicti slugs stop moving and undergo a transformation into plantlike organisms. In place of the original slugs now stand rigid, immobile "plants" that resemble very small caramel apples on tiny sticks. Spores form inside the "apple" part and burst through to the outside when mature. These spores with their tough cell walls resemble fungi and feed on decaying plant material. Eventually, each spore gives rise to an individual amoeba and the dicti life cycle begins again. I vividly remember an inventive college professor giving me and two hundred other students petri plates with dicti ameoba cells. I took mine back to the dorm and watched spellbound as slugs mysteriously sprang up from microscopic cells and then turned into little balls and sticks. For years I thought that if only dicti were one hundred times larger with a taste for human flesh, it would make a horrific science fiction menace.

While dicti slugs are harmless, the same cannot be said of the black cancer organisms in "Tunguska." Scully finds a colony of black vermiform (wormlike) organisms attached to Dr. Sacks's pineal gland, located just north of the hypothalamus in the brain. The pineal gland was historically viewed as the "seat of the soul" for its role in neurological and psychiatric disorders. One might think that the presence of vermiform creatures nesting in the pineal gland and paralysis imply cause-and-effect, but one would be wrong. Lab rats seem to live quite happily with their pineal glands removed. One dead giveaway that the black cancer creatures are cohabiting a human body is a black slimy film that appears over the eyes of the host. Since the pineal gland is directly connected by nerves to the eyes, the black film could be disrupting the perception of light by the host's pineal gland, thereby affecting the behavior of the host. In the *X-Files* episode "Piper Maru," infection by the same alien organism led to strange behaviors on the part of the human hosts, almost as if they were possessed by an occupying force.

Another major function of the pineal gland is to ensure that mammals without access to desktop calendars give birth during spring and summer, when the weather is nice and food is abundant. To synchronize the best times for romantic flings, mammals can unconsciously sense the time of the year by how long the sun is out during the day. Daylight is perceived by the eye's retina, which is connected by nerve cells to the pineal gland. The gland secretes the chemical melatonin, which controls fertility in females and the sex drive in males. It's not just rats and mice that obey their pineal glands and give birth during nice weather. Statistics for human births also indicate that more babies are born in spring and summer than in fall and winter. Unfortunately, Dr. Sacks is killed before Scully can complete her analysis on the connection between the pineal gland and the strange worms.

EXT. RURAL AREA (TUNGUSKA, RUSSIA)—DAY

KRYCEK
Tell me what we're doing here.

Mulder stops digging now, too. Looks at Krycek. There's a moment where we wonder if he might not rabbit punch him again. Then:

MULDER
June 30, 1908. Tungus tribesmen and Russian fur traders

looked up into the southeastern Siberian sky and saw a fire-
ball streaking to earth. When it hit the atmosphere it created a series of cataclysmic explosions that are considered
the largest cosmic event in the history of civilization. Two
thousand times the force of the A-bomb dropped on Hiroshima.

Mulder continues to dig.

                          KRYCEK

What was it?

                          MULDER

It's been speculated that it was a piece of a comet or an asteroid, even a piece of anti-matter. The power of the blast
felled trees in a radial pattern over an area of two thousand kilometers. But no real definitive evidence has ever
been found to satisfy an explanation. Of what it was.

Mulder has moved enough earth to slip under the fence now. As Krycek
watches him crawl to the other side.

                          MULDER

I think someone found that evidence. And I think the explanation might be something no one ever dreamed.

                                          —"Tunguska"

Meanwhile, Mulder travels to Russia to search for the origin of
the meteorite containing the alien organism. After trekking through
the remote wilderness of Siberia, he finds workers unearthing a huge
meteorite in the Tunguska region. Mulder would most certainly understand the significance of finding a meteorite in this location. Tunguska is the site of the largest natural explosion in the history of
civilization.

At 7:17 A.M. on June 30, 1908, local tribesmen in the trading
post of Vanivara in Siberia saw a ball of fire blazing across the cloudless sky followed by a deafening explosion. Whatever occurred four
to five miles above the rolling hills and forests of the Tunguska river

region released a blast of energy straight downward that was two thousand times greater than the atomic bomb that devastated Hiroshima. Seismographs from around the world picked up pressure waves from an event so catastrophic that the waves circled the Earth twice. Trees, more than 60 million, toppled over in an area the size of Rhode Island. Fiery lights flickered for days afterward, illuminating midnight skies all over Europe and Asia. The lights were so bright that citizens of London thought that their city was on fire. Although the event probably devastated reindeer herds in the isolated region, only two people died. Tunguska is so remote that it took nineteen years for the first Russian expedition to reach the devastated site. Even today, visiting the site means a fifty-mile hike if a convenient helicopter is not available.

Roy Gallant, director of the Southworth Planetarium at the University of Maine, was the first American to visit Tunguska. Roy told me that it takes an experienced eye to see any remaining traces of the catastrophe. Directly beneath where the explosion occurred stands a forest of telephone poles—sixty-foot trees stripped of their branches that are stark reminders of the downward force of the blast. Remains of other trees three to ten miles away lie on the forest floor in a radial pattern pointing outward from the center of the cataclysm. Otherwise, there are no craters, no signs of further disruption to a landscape that must have once looked like ground zero after an atomic blast.

There are two mainstream explanations for what caused the explosion in Tunguska. One group of scientists led by Chris Chyba, Peter Thomas, and Kevin Zahnle are convinced that minute rock fragments buried in trees point to the explosion of a stony meteor measuring fifty to sixty yards in diameter. Others, including Roy Gallant, believe that only a comet weighing in at over 100,000 tons could explain the mysterious lights that preceded the event by several days. Mulder would probably favor one of the more unusual explanations—a nuclear explosion from a crashed UFO or passage of a black hole through the Earth. However, a little scientific investigation by Scully would fail to find a trace of radioactive material in the region. She also would conclude that a black hole would have exited through the fishing grounds of Newfoundland, Canada. Why no fisherman bothered reporting the deafening explosion of a black hole shooting out of the ocean or the immense tidal wave that followed are questions that somehow haven't deterred the black hole enthusiasts. According to the *X-Files* episode "Tunguska," if scientists had dug in the right place or at the correct depth they would have found the real culprit—a huge black meteorite filled with the alien black cancer organism.

In "Tunguska" and the earlier episode "Ice," meteors are the delivery systems for alien hitchhikers that are able to invade a human host. This brings up several very interesting questions. What are the chances that an alien microbe could survive a trip through space on a vehicle that lacks such basic amenities as an atmosphere, temperature control, sunscreen, refreshments, and brakes? And providing that an organism could survive the rather abrupt explosion or crash landing at the end of the flight, what are the chances that it could become a parasite of Earth's creatures?

Let's first consider whether a microbe could survive an interstellar cruise on a rock. You might be surprised to learn that respected scientists have been asking this rather unusual question for nearly 100 years. At the turn of the twentieth century, a Swedish electrolyte chemist named Svante Arrhenius wondered if bacteria could survive in outer space. His curiosity on this subject must have earned him many puzzled looks and raised eyebrows from colleagues. Arrhenius's delving into the realm of science fiction was spurred by a discovery that seems at first glance to be unrelated to space-faring microbes—he found that light can exert a force on objects, if the objects are very, very small. Arrhenius observed that clouds of tiny particles blasted off the icy core of a comet are swept back away from the sun like sails in a solar breeze. That is, light waves exert enough force to push small ice particles, like wind pushing the leaves of a tree. As a physical chemist, Arrhenius determined mathematically that objects would need to be between the size of a bacterial spore and a tiny dust particle to be moved by light. Therefore, Arrhenius speculated, if bacteria could survive in space, they could sail between the stars powered by gentle solar breezes.

At first glance, bacteria in space seems like a fantasy worthy of Mulder's imagination. The hardships bacteria would need to overcome seem overwhelming. If the microbes don't die of asphyxiation or dehydration then the intense cold of near absolute zero should turn their cellular liquid into jagged ice spears. Microbes would have as much chance surviving floating freely in space as they would have surviving being stranded on the moon.

But bacteria *can* survive being stranded on the moon. In 1967, the unmanned lunar lander *Surveyor 3* set down gently on the surface of the moon and sent back detailed pictures of a future manned landing site. The cameras of *Surveyor 3* remained on the moon for two and a half years before being picked up by *Apollo 12* astronauts and returned to Earth. NASA scientists were astonished to find that tiny bacteria had stowed away in the camera before *Surveyor 3* was launched from Earth. These bacteria survived their odyssey with no water and after repeated cycles of being frozen and thawed, courtesy of the moon's huge monthly temperature swings. Pete Conrad, commander of the *Apollo 12* mission, considered the survival of the wayward bacteria to be the most significant finding of the mission. In retrospect, Pete might not have been surprised at the hardiness of bacteria had he known what Arrhenius knew—bacterial spores can withstand desiccation in a powerful vacuum and still grow and reproduce afterward.

Surviving in a frigid vacuum is only one hurdle to overcome. If bacteria are to survive the rigors of unprotected space, they must live through constant buffeting by deadly cosmic rays and ultraviolet radiation. These high-energy emissions from the sun make mincemeat of DNA and other essential molecules by blasting apart chemical bonds. Bacteria should have as much chance surviving the intense radiation of interstellar space as they would have surviving in extremely radioactive water surrounding the core of a nuclear power plant.

You guessed it. There are bacteria living in radioactive water inside nuclear power plants. The appropriately named *Micrococcus radiophilus* manages to exist in conditions that would instantly kill a human and even turn glass brown and crumbly. Bacteria such as *Micrococcus radiophilus* have evolved several ingenious strategies for withstanding exposure to radiation. The first line of defense is a shell made of sugar and protein that surrounds a bacterium's fragile plasma membrane. The protective nature of the shell can be increased with a dark pigment that acts like sunscreen and is used by bacteria that live in the upper atmosphere. Bacteria also have a task force of enzymes that constantly monitor and repair errors and damage in their DNA. Why, some scientists argue, have bacteria evolved such abilities if not to cruise the heavens?

So it is not outside the realm of extreme possibility that cells might survive on meteors such as the one portrayed in "Tunguska." Proponents of this theory go on to speculate that life on Earth may have originated from microbes landing from outer space. This theory of the origin of life was first voiced by Arrhenius, who called the idea *panspermia*. Believers in panspermia contend that life did not develop on Earth but was seeded by bacteria from outer space. Panspermia, proponents suggest, is the only answer to the question of how life could have originated from nonlife in less than—perhaps considerably less than—750 million years. Like Mulder, panspermia proponents suggest that aliens might be invading all the time as stowaways on comets, meteroids, or space dust. Believers in panspermia are not just science fiction junkies. Francis Crick (Nobel laureate and co-discoverer of the structure of DNA) supports the theory of panspermia as does noted English astronomer Sir Fred Hoyle. Even Dana Scully, in "Biogenesis," the last episode of the sixth season, concedes that panspermia is a plausible hypothesis. Because it is accepted that bacteria can survive under conditions once thought impossible, debates on the possibility of panspermia now appear in major scientific magazines.

How much life might be cruising the galaxy, hitching rides on comets or sailing on dust? Quite a bit, according to Fred Hoyle. Hoyle, with his colleague Chandra Wickramasinghe, made this highly controversial assertion in 1979 while studying a curious cosmic phenomenon—galactic dust clouds. First a little history: In the 1920s, the spectrum of light reflected by galactic dust clouds indicated that water was a major dust cloud component. By the 1950s, more sensitive instruments revealed a host of other substances. But what? Hoyle and Wickramasinghe suspected that dust clouds contained a mixture of water and some carbon compounds, possibly graphite (like pencil lead). They tried various mixtures of ice and graphite in the laboratory to see if they could re-create the same peaks and valleys of the light spectrum reflecting off the dust clouds, without success. Another baffling mystery was that only nearly hollow particles of about one micrometer in size could explain a discrepancy between the light diffracted by the clouds and their apparent mass. The puzzle seemed impossible to solve.

For years, Hoyle and Wickramasinghe pondered their riddle. What was mostly water and carbon, with a dash of other common elements thrown in, hollow, and about a micrometer in size? In 1979, the answer hit them: bacteria. In the laboratory, bacteria fit the spectrum of light bouncing off the dust clouds perfectly. Needless to say, the declaration of Hoyle and Wickramasinghe that clouds of bacteria are sailing through the galaxy provoked an outpouring of criticism— but no one has yet to provide another answer for the riddle of the galactic dust clouds.

So there are structures resembling fossils of microbes in meteorites and evidence that bacteria could survive a trip through space. However, other interpretations of the evidence are also possible. Deep down, like Scully, I will only be convinced when a sample is retrieved off a comet or planet and life is found that could not possibly have originated from Earthly contamination.

Missions are now being planned to do precisely that—to retrieve samples from other planets. One of the most likely places in the solar system where life may exist is Europa, Jupiter's smallest moon. Europa is one of the most brilliant objects in the solar system. Its flat surface reflects light off a shimmering layer of ice. The *Galileo* space probe recently traveled so close to the surface that cameras could have picked up a vacation cottage. While such obvious signs of life are unlikely given the frigid -260 degree Fahrenheit surface temperature, pictures provided tantalizing evidence that conditions below the surface may be suitable for living creatures. Photographs show striation patterns indicating that the ice sheet had been broken and rebroken many times—signs that a turbulent liquid ocean once flowed and might still flow beneath the ice. Other experiments on board *Galileo* indicate that both Europa and its sister moon Callisto have interiors that are able to conduct electricity. The most likely explanation? The electrical conductor is a substance contained in liquid water. The very strong possibility of liquid water means that the internal temperature of the moons are sufficiently warm to create an ocean of water.

The likeliest heat source so far from the sun is the internal friction of the moon itself moving over a molten core, the same tectonic motion on Earth that frees heat vents in the ocean floor. Since on Earth thermophilic (heat-loving) bacteria thrive around such vents at temperatures above the boiling point of water—more evidence, if such were needed, for the ubiquity of life on, in, and under the earth's surface—similar life on Europa appears more and more probable. There is even an atmosphere, with a smattering of oxygen molecules.

Missions are already being planned that will answer the question of whether life is present below the surface of Jupiter's glowing moon. Determining whether the ocean still exists will require landing a probe on the surface, a mission that NASA is studying for the early twenty-first century. The search for life, however, requires more creativity. One plan is to send a pencil-shaped robot that will plunge itself into the ice and deliver an aquabot that will search and report back. Another idea is to send a spacecraft that will orbit Europa and drop a boron-nitride bomb on the ice. The explosion will send up a plume of chunks and chips that can be grabbed when the craft flies through it.

If life is found below the surface of Europa or Mars, would it be similar to life on our planet? Would it share the same biochemistry as ours? The answer depends on the validity of theories like panspermia. If there was a single genesis of life in our solar system, then cells on other planets may share common characteristics with life on Earth, such as DNA for the genetic material and being surrounded by plasma membranes. Some divergence from terrestrial life would certainly be found since life on other planets would be shaped by different environmental conditions. However, bacteria that have lived below our own ground for hundreds of millions of years survive in environments completely unlike the habitats of bacteria above ground, yet these deep dwellers are remarkably similar to their aboveground cousins. A few simple experiments such as those performed by Dr. Carpenter on the contents of the Erlenmeyer flask should be sufficient to establish whether a relationship exists between any cells from Europa and cells from Earth.

There is a possibility that if alien bacteria shared a single genesis with our bacteria, they could have a harmful effect on human physiology. For this reason, stringent containment measures are planned for any rocks returned to Earth. However, the odds should not be any greater than for random Earth bacteria to be pathogenic on humans. Of the countless species of bacteria on our planet, very few are harmful.

    INT. ARCTIC COMPOUND—NIGHT
    MICROSCOPE MATTE

If a single celled creature could appear mean and vicious, this is it. Protective spikes encircle the undulating membrane. A whip-like flagellum propels the creature in an excited state.

                    MURPHY (O.S.)
        Tell me that's not a foreign object.

    WIDER

Mulder pulls away. Scully looks into the tube. What she sees seems to take her breath away. Scully looks to Mulder.

                    SCULLY
        The same thing is in Richter's blood.

Everyone tenses. She gestures to her work area. Mulder moves to the other microscope. Bear watches intently, nervous, as Mulder peers into the tube.

    MICROSCOPE MATTE

Indeed, the same kind of creature is moving about.

    WIDER

Mulder pulls up from the scope. Scully turns to the others.

                    SCULLY
        That single celled organism could be the larval stage of a
        larger animal.

                    HODGE
        That's a big leap, Scully.

SCULLY

The evidence is there.

—"Ice"

If alien life-forms were unrelated to terrestrial life, could they still be harmful? This would depend on the biochemistry of the alien organism (and whether they have ray guns). For example, let's speculate about the biochemistry of the weaponless alien worm in the *X-Files* episode "Ice." The worm was discovered in an ice-core sample that was retrieved from deep below the ice of northern Alaska near a meteorite. The ice surrounding the worm contains high levels of ammonia. Mulder speculates that the alien worm originated on a planet with an ammonium atmosphere.

There are many qualities of ammonia that make it ripe for extraterrestrial speculation. Such speculation usually begins with an awareness of the importance of liquid water to life on Earth. Water's structural properties (and omnipresence) are so important to every form of earth-based life that most scientists believe that extraterrestrial life is likely to be found only on planets where water exists in its liquid form. As this represents a fairly narrow range of temperatures—32 degrees to 212 degrees F—the number of possible planets is similarly restricted . . . that is, unless a substance like water can be found. Consider, therefore, ammonia.

Ammonia consists of a nitrogen atom bonded with three hydrogen atoms. Water is an oxygen atom bonded with two hydrogens. Both molecules are polar. This means that the electrons shared between atoms forming a chemical bond are not shared equally. The electrons are more strongly attracted to the nitrogen or the oxygen and therefore spend less time with the bonded hydrogens. Since electrons have a negative charge, by spending more time with the oxygen or nitrogen than the hydrogens, the oxygen and nitrogen have a more negative charge and the hydrogens are more positively charged. Since negative- and positive-charged atoms attract, the more positive hydrogens are attracted to atoms on other molecules that have a more negative charge. The polar property of water—the "universal solvent"—is why it can dissolve proteins, salts, and sugars. Since ammonia is also polar, the essential position of water as the liquid of life on Earth would be filled by ammonia on an ammonium world.

On our temperate planet, ammonia evaporates at room temperature, which is what accounts for its strong odor. If it were much colder and the atmosphere was soaked with ammonia, ammonia would form pools of liquid just like water. Imagine then an ammonia planet: freezing cold with oceans of ammonia. Mulder is correct in stating that if the worm's planet had an ammonium atmosphere, it would have to be a frigid place. Based simply on outside temperature, the worm would feel right at home in the ice of northern Alaska.

Could life develop on a planet with an ammonium atmosphere? Where water is scarce and liquid ammonia is abundant? Possibly. Imagine a world where the primordial soup is mainly ammonia with a dash of carbon dioxide, phosphate, and some metals. Substitute water for ammonia, and conditions might be similar to Earth's during the dawn of life. The ammonia world would need an energy source, say UV light radiating from a nearby star. Our virgin ammonia planet would be a beautiful place. Yellowish-orange oceans of ammonia shimmering beneath a thick, gaseous atmosphere of ammonia, nitrogen, and carbon dioxide. Lightning storms would deliver torrents of ammonia rain to the surface.

Within a few billion years, the first life-forms could evolve on the planet: tiny, single-cell microbes capable of using the sun's energy to build the complex molecules of life—microbes capable of photosynthesis. On our water world, the sun's energy powers the photosynthetic conversion of water and carbon dioxide into oxygen and sugars. On the ammonium world, photosynthetic microbes could use their sun's energy to convert ammonia into nitrate, by replacing the hydrogens bonded to the nitrogen in ammonia with oxygens. At the same time carbon dioxide would be converted into sugars. New microbes could evolve that feed on the photosynthetic microbes, which eventually could lead to a type of eukaryotic cell.

Creatures of an ammonium world would probably be carbon based. Advanced organisms would eat food rich in nitrate and carbohydrates (sugars). They would breathe in nitrogen and exhale carbon dioxide. The alien worms from an ammonium planet would probably drool at the sight of freshly fertilized plants, since plants are filled with carbohydrates and fertilizer contains nitrates. If the alien worms proved unfriendly, guns and bombs would not be required, just a garden hose. Water would be as noxious a poison to them as ammonia is to us.

On our water-based world, ammonia is a household product handy for killing bacteria. Ammonia is toxic because, just like water, it passes through the plasma membranes of cells. When ammonia gets into bacteria and fungal cells, it acts like drain cleaner, causing instant death. Water should have the same effect on ammonia-based creatures. The worms from the episode "Ice," if they originated on an ammonium-soaked world, would be poisoned by water long before they ever reached the brain. No creature from an ammonia-based planet could ever be a parasite of a water-based organism.

Whether or not you believe in alien hitchhikers, three hundred tons of extraterrestrial organic matter fall to Earth every year courtesy of comets, meteors, and dust. Four billion years ago, when life on Earth was first appearing, there were hundreds or thousands of times as many comets and meteors on collision courses with Earth. William Irvine, a University of Massachusetts astronomer, estimates that enough comets, meteorites, and dust have fallen over the years of Earth's existence to provide all the raw organic materials present on the planet. Life may or may not have originated on our planet, but our molecules are nevertheless the molecules of the universe.

Sea Urchins in the Arctic

INT. MULDER'S APARTMENT—EARLY MORNING

SCULLY

I have come here today, four years later, to report to you on the illegitimacy of Agent Mulder's work. That it is my scientific opinion he became, through the course of these years, a victim of his own false hopes, and of his belief in the biggest of lies.

According to Fox Mulder, proof of the existence of extraterrestrial life would be the greatest discovery in the history of science. It is the holy grail of his life, the search for his sister, kidnapped during a terrifying evening of bright lights when they were both children. In "Gethsemane," the final episode of the fourth season, Mulder be-

lieves that he has finally found the elusive proof. A Canadian geo-
detic survey team, which specializes in mapping land while taking
into account the curvature of the earth's surface, finds a body frozen
in the wall of an ice cave. It looks like the quintessential alien: small
stature, large bald head, wide oval eyes, gray wrinkled skin, and in-
determinate sex . . . another of the "grays," an alien body that fits the
description given by numerous "abductees" and Roswell, New Mexico, "eyewitnesses." If it is a hoax, it is a deadly serious one. When an
excited Mulder finally reaches the remote site, he is greeted by the
bullet-riddled bodies of the survey team. Fortunately, the frozen
alien was hidden by the one surviving member. After returning to
civilization, an autopsy of the body reveals masses of stringy white
tissue not found in normal humans.

Mulder believes that the alien corpse is authentic while Scully is
skeptical. Besides the body, the only hard evidence is in the form of ice-
core samples taken from the cave. If the ice-core samples prove to be at
least two hundred years old, the last time that the cave was not covered
with ice, then a body near the ice samples should also date from the
same time. Since people in the eighteenth century probably weren't
squirreling away fake aliens in the Arctic, the date that the body was
frozen would be an important clue in establishing the truth.

At Mulder's request, Scully takes the ice samples to Dr.
Vitagliano at the Exobiology Laboratory, Goddard Space Center. At
first glance, the samples are just what would be expected for ice that
has not melted for hundreds of years—layers of sedimentation with
the surface layer containing hydrocarbon pollutants that not even
the Arctic can escape. No surprises, until Dr. Vitagliano analyzes the
ice sample more closely. Using a light microscope, he sees that within
the ice matrix are cells. When Dr. Vitagliano tells Scully that cells are
in the ice, she asks if the cells are from a plant or animal. His answer
is cryptic. The cells cannot be classified as plant or animal.

Scully is surprised by Dr. Vitagliano's response because she
knows that plant and animal cells are easy to differentiate. Only
plant cells have a sturdy rectangular wall composed of proteins and
sugars that surrounds the plasma membrane. Plant cells also have
chloroplasts, the little cell-like organelles that help make sugars from
sunlight, water, and carbon dioxide. Taking up much of the interior
space in some plant cells is an enormous bubble called a vacuole, the

storage bin and waste pit of the cell. Finally, plant cells do not have little cubicles called lysosomes, which are used by animal cells for storing enzymes that would be detrimental if floating around free. Besides these differences, which are easily observable using a light microscope, plant and animal cells are remarkably similar. Both have nuclei containing the DNA genome and a main compartment within which float membranes, ribosomes, mitochondria, and other constituents.

For the cells to be unclassifiable, they must have a mixture of plant and animal features. Since such cells do not exist in nature and are not shown on camera, let's be imaginative and speculate. Dr. Vitagliano may be looking at cells that lack a cell wall and contain lysosomes like animal cells while having organelles that look like chloroplasts and a large vacuole. Alternatively, the cells could have a cell wall but be completely animal-like within the plasma membrane. When Chris Carter was writing this episode, he phoned to ask what he should call cells that are a mixture of two organisms. I told Chris that these are known as hybrid cells, or chimeras. The word *chimera* dates back to a creature from Greek mythology, a fire-breathing monster with a lion's head, a goat's body, and a serpent's tail. When I received the script to check it for accuracy, I was amused to see that Chris had used both terms, calling the cells "chimerical hybrids." Chris and I had several conversations about hybrid cells over the years, beginning with the episode "The Host," which contained a charming chimeric organism known as flukeman.

Chris was intrigued to learn that any two cells can be fused together providing that they both have plasma membranes at their outermost surfaces. For plant cells, this means removing the protein-sugar wall that encloses the plasma membrane. The reason why any two cells can be fused is that proteins and lipids move freely within a membrane, making the membrane a highly fluid structure. Bring two cells together, and the membranes flow into each other, much like two drops of liquid mercury can coalesce to become a single large drop. Hybrid cells can result from the fusion of different types of cells from the same organism, say muscle and liver cells, or from the fusion of cells from two different organisms, like humans and aliens. On my suggestion, Chris made the fusion of fluke and human cells one of the possibilities for how flukeman was generated.

Science defines hybrid organisms as the progeny of parents that normally would choose not to intermingle, like man and fluke. Distinct species of organisms arise because members either cannot or will not breed with other organisms. While plants can form fertile hybrids between species, even between genera—some highly decorative orchids are derived from as many as four different genera—hybrid animals are rare and sterile. Organism development is a complicated process and both genomes of a hybrid organism must work closely together, which is not usually possible. Mules are the best-known animal hybrids, the natural offspring of male donkeys and female horses. Beefalo, a new hybrid animal whose meat is available in my supermarket, is produced from crossing cows and buffalo. Creatures like flukeman and human-animal hybrids in fictional stories like H. G. Wells's *The Island of Dr. Moreau* are pure fantasy.

While Scully and Dr. Vitagliano are puzzling over the strange hybrid cells, Mulder's belief in the authenticity of the alien body is shaken when he is told by a Department of Defense employee named Kritschgau that he has been fooled by an elaborate hoax. The body, Kritschgau tells him, is really an artificial creation from the genetic manipulation of chimeric cells. What Kritschgau seems to be stating is that the alien is merely a strange-looking hybrid, cleverly concocted in a laboratory from cells of two natural terrestrial organisms. This would make the alien simply a modern science version of Piltdown Man.

Piltdown Man is the most famous fraud in the history of science. The hoax began in 1912 when amateur archaeologist Charles Dawson discovered fragments of a skull in the Piltdown quarry in Sussex, England. The skull was a tremendous boost for English anthropologists, who felt left out after Continental scientists discovered Neanderthal, Cro-Magnon, and Java Man remains. Piltdown Man outshone all other finds. It was the "missing link," a humanlike skull with elephantlike teeth and an apelike jaw. And that's what it was. A human skull, elephant molars, and an orangutan jaw.

The perpetrators of the hoax were very clever. The teeth were filed to fit the jaw. The skull was broken to obscure the nonexistent connection with the jaw. The bones were boiled and treated with an iron solution to make them look old. When scientists voiced doubts that the jawbone and skull seemed to be from different animals that coincidentally died in the same location, a new skull and jaw were miraculously found. One such coincidence, maybe. Two? It had to be from the same creature. For forty years, anthropologists puzzled over Piltdown Man, the only anomaly in the increasingly fleshed-out theory on the evolution of man. The hoax survived until a new fluorine dating test in 1949 established that the skull was merely six hundred years old and the jaw was twentieth-century ape. Still, it took another four years before a paper was published establishing the nature of the hoax.

Just like Mulder can be fooled by an alien hoax because he so desperately wants to believe, British anthropologists accepted the lie because it was precisely what they wanted to find. At the time, the leading theory of man's evolution was that the braincase would develop before the jaw, leading to a humanlike skull and a simian jaw. Piltdown Man fit the theory perfectly. The British were also pleased because finding Piltdown Man in England meant that the first intelligent humans were, of course, British. Another reason why the Piltdown Man fraud was so easily perpetrated was that none of the principals seemed to have anything to gain. No one became rich over the finding, although reputations were certainly enhanced. Amazing scientific discoveries made by reputable people don't usually elicit accusations of fraud. What the anthropologists needed at the time was an objective scientist like Scully with access to the bones. Someone who would have taken better X rays, tested both the skull and the jaw for similar organic matter, and used a microscope on the teeth to discover the very obvious signs of tampering.

The perpetrators of the Piltdown Man hoax remain a mystery. Was it Charles Dawson, the finder of the "fossils" and now known to be a notorious forger and plagiarizer? Or perhaps it was Sir Arthur Woodward, the Keeper of Geology of the British Museum's Natural History Department who had access to bone collections that could be used to fake the remains. Teilhard de Chardin, before he became a prominent theologian, accompanied Dawson and Woodward into the field, and has since been accused—if that's the correct word—by Harvard paleontologist Stephen Jay Gould. Even Sir Arthur Conan Doyle, famous writer of the Sherlock Holmes mysteries, has come under suspicion since he lived in the area.

When Mulder asks Kritschgau why people would want to perpetrate an alien hoax, he replies that the lie is there to divert attention from greater lies. Mulder responds that science today is quite capable of testing the body to discover the truth. But before testing can begin, the body is stolen. The question remains unanswered: Is it real, or is it an elaborate hoax?

If the body had not been stolen, Kritschgau's information that the alien was just a chimera of known terrestrial species could easily have been tested. Over the years, Mulder and Scully have frequently relied on DNA analysis to help determine if strange-looking corpses were man, ape, or alien. DNA can be used as a precise fingerprint because every organism on Earth, except for identical twins and clones, has its own unique genome. The precise order of the 6 billion nucleotides in your genome is a mixture of your parents' genomes. If you were to compare your nucleotide order with that of any other person's, they would differ by only about 0.1 percent, which is still a considerable 6 million nucleotides.[8] If your DNA is only 98.5 percent the same as the DNA of humans, you would be swinging through the trees with your fellow chimps.

If someone commits a crime and leaves a trace of themselves behind—a wisp of hair, a drop of blood, a flake of skin—then DNA in these samples can be matched to the perpetrator's DNA. The current ability to match a sample of DNA to the person it came from requires the identification of regions of the human genome that tend to vary among people, the so-called variable regions. The chances that two people will have exactly the same DNA sequence in ten different variable regions is as low as one in several billion. Variable regions of DNA, most of which have no known function, tend to be located in between genes. The reason for variability in nonfunctional DNA regions is simple. Nucleotide changes, also called mutations, can accumulate in nonfunctional parts of the genome over the millions of years of human existence without harm. In the same way, bad sectors that accumulate in unused portions of a computer's hard drive are substantially less damaging than bad sectors in the operating sys-

---

[8]As psychologist and philosopher William James put it, "There is very little difference between one man and another, but what difference there is, is very important."

tem of the computer. Genes have to specify the building of a precise protein. Mutations in the DNA of a gene can seriously affect the composition and function of the specified protein. Acquire a new mutation in an important gene and the individual might never develop normally enough to be born.

The most common test to match DNA samples is called restriction fragment length polymorphism, or RFLP. When Mulder and Scully talk about the need to conduct DNA analysis on a sample of human blood or tissue, this is usually what they mean. The RFLP test was used in the O. J. Simpson murder trial to determine whose blood was on objects of evidence. It was also used to identify the remains of the Romanovs, the Russian imperial family murdered in 1917, whose bones lay hidden for seventy years.

The RFLP test makes use of natural bacterial enzymes called restriction enzymes, which recognize small sequence patterns in DNA. For example, the enzyme called EcoRI recognizes the nucleotide sequence GAATTC (guanine-adenine-adenine-thymine-thymine-cytosine). The enzyme will snip the DNA double helix wherever this order of nucleotides appears. If GAATTC is found once in a piece of DNA, then the enzyme will cut the DNA at its location, resulting in two pieces of DNA. In a DNA chain that is millions of nucleotides long, the sequence GAATTC will appear many times and the DNA will be cut into many pieces after treatment with the enzyme.

In a variable region of the DNA, not all people will have the same order of nucleotides. If the sequence GAATTC appears in a variable region of the DNA, then the DNA of some people might be slightly different. Instead of GAATTC, some people might have TAATTC. The DNA of people with TAATTC will no longer be cut at this location by the EcoRI enzyme. Since the fragments of DNA after enzyme treatment are separated according to their size, people will have different sizes and numbers of fragments depending on whether the enzymes cut or didn't cut the DNA at a particular place. To perfectly match a human DNA sample with a particular person, a variety of different restriction enzymes that each recognize a different short sequence of DNA are used to examine a number of different variable regions of the genome.

RFLP analysis is useful if you need to identify a specific person. To determine if tissue is human, ape, alien, or some weird chimera, it is easier to simply determine the order of nucleotides in a particular region of DNA. The nucleotide order in the ribosomal DNA sequence has already been determined for thousands of organisms. By sequencing this gene from the DNA of an unknown creature, you can immediately identify its origin or determine if it has a known close relative. Just as (the late) Dr. Anne Carpenter sequenced the ribosomal DNA gene to determine the nature of the unknown bacteria in the episode "The Erlenmeyer Flask," sequencing the ribosomal DNA gene from a sample of the "fake" alien's tissue would tell a scientist the organism from which the tissue came.

Mulder tells Scully that despite Kritschgau's tale of alien hoaxes, he is still inclined to believe that the alien body is genuine. Scully informs Mulder that the chimeric cells found in the ice matrix support Kritschgau's story of how the fake alien was engineered in the lab. Mulder argues that the chimeric cells could be extraterrestrial. Scientifically, Mulder has a point. Kritschgau's explanation that chimeric cells were used to construct the alien indicates a technology that is well beyond what science can accomplish on this planet.

In the *X-Files* episode "Redux," the sequel to "Gethsemane," Dr. Vitagliano continues his tests on the chimeric cells from the ice-core sample to determine if they are capable of cell division. In other words, he wants to determine if the cells are still living. For real hybrid cells to be capable of cell division, their parent cells must be closely related, like mice and humans. Chris Carter, who wrote the episode, wanted to know how Dr. Vitagliano could discover that not only were the chimeric cells alive, but that they were developing into an organism. I told Chris that Dr. Vitagliano should place the cells in a nutrient-rich solution. If these were normal animal cells, he would use a pink-colored liquid broth enriched with fetal bovine serum. Dr. Vitagliano tells Scully that when he placed the cells in the media, the cells began to divide.

. Since Scully would know that media containing baby cow blood would not please even a carnivorous plant, she assumes that the cells must be from an animal. Dr. Vitagliano still maintains that the cells cannot be classified. Scully is confused, and tells him that the cells were able to complete mitotic cell division in the media.

Eukaryotic cells can divide either by mitotic cell division (mitosis) or meiotic cell division (meiosis). Whether the cells are chimeras from the Arctic or parts of your lung, nearly all will divide by mitosis. In mitosis, one cell becomes two, and the two daughter cells are perfect copies of the parent cell. Many of the 100 trillion hardworking cells in your body have very short life spans. One cell dividing to give two is the only way to replace the billions of cells in your body that die every day so that you can live. Skin cells last only between one and thirty-four days and the cells lining your stomach give out after only two days. Not happy with your current liver? If the cells are healthy and able to divide, you'll have a new liver every five hundred days. Some cells in your body don't divide and cannot be replaced. Nerve cells, such as your brain cells, and heart muscle cells are designed to last a lifetime, but the manufacturer's warranty doesn't cover self-destructive activities.

Only cells called germ cells, which give rise to egg and sperm sex cells, divide by the process called meiosis. In meiosis, daughter cells end up with exactly half the DNA of the parent germ cell. This way, when egg and sperm cells join together, they each contribute half of the DNA to the composite cell, called a zygote. From a single cell, the zygote starts mitotic cell division and develops into a complete organism.

Since the ice-core sample cells don't appear to be germ cells, they must divide by mitosis, as Scully suggests. Scully expects the cells to divide like average animal cells would if bathed in nutrient media—the two daughter cells separate completely from each other after the division. Instead, she is shocked to learn from Dr. Vitagliano that when the cells started dividing, they began to go through the stages of morula, blastula, and gastrula.

I explained to Chris how Dr. Vitagliano could tell that the cells were developing into a complex life-form. In many animals, after the sperm cell fertilizes the egg cell to form a zygote, the zygote starts mitosis and the resulting glob of cells goes through defined stages of development that can be easily identified using a light microscope. Morula, blastula, and gastrula are three of the early developmental stages. Only animal zygote cells have the complete genetic program and activated cytoplasm necessary to proceed through the many stages of organism development. In plants, it's different. While normally a plant develops from a zygote, which is produced when pollen fertilizes an ovule, I had talked to Chris about how I had taken ordinary plant cells and tricked them into believing that they were really "zygotes." The cells proceeded to go through the many stages of plant embryo development. This type of development, which does not begin with a real zygote, is called somatic development. The term "somatic" refers to the type of cell undergoing development. All cells of an organism that are not germ cells are somatic cells.

Scully and Dr. Vitagliano agree that the cells have begun somatic development, which will eventually result in a life-form. For this scene, Chris needed a real live alien organism. Since one was not readily available, he asked for my help. What could he use that would look alien and wouldn't be easily recognized by the average *X-Files* fan? Tough question. After mulling the possibilities with my scientist husband, Cliff, for several hours, we agreed on our alien—a pluteus, one of the stages in the development of the common sea urchin. And I knew just where Chris could film a pluteus. One of the foremost labs studying sea urchin development was a stone's throw away from 20th Century Fox, the home of Chris's Ten Thirteen Production Company: Eric Davidson's lab at the California Institute of Technology.

When the audience is treated to a view through the microscope of the developing alien, they see the pluteus, a translucent, pulsing creature with several protrusions coming from one end and a pointed other end. Scully and Dr. Vitagliano are mesmerized by the creature, and with luck, so was the audience. I wondered at the time if any viewers would recognize that the alien creature was really a sea urchin. The next day, I received an answer. A faculty member friend told me that she watched the episode with her husband, a novice *X-Files* viewer and scientist who studies marine organisms. After the scene where the pluteus "alien" is shown, he turned to my friend and with a puzzled look on his face asked, "What are sea urchins doing in the Arctic?"

In "Gethsemane" and "Redux," as well as "The Erlenmeyer Flask" and "Tunguska," aliens are not little green men or costumed monsters, but something far more sophisticated . . . and plausible. The aliens are cells. If we are fortunate enough to discover life on Mars or Europa, it is cells that will be brought back to Earth for study. As a scientist, I shiver with anticipation when I think about that hypothetical test tube in the containment room at Fort Detrick. Will cells be found? Will they prove that life in our solar system had a single genesis? And if not, what strange metabolism will these cells have? What type of genetic material? Will they have plasma membranes? Will they have the same twenty amino acids in their proteins as on Earth? My questions are endless. Aliens do not have to step out of spaceships saying, "I come in peace," or blow up the White House to be worthy of our attention. I agree with Mulder. Proof of the existence of extraterrestrial life would be the greatest discovery in the history of science.

It would make for pretty compelling television, too.

3

Mutants and Monsters

Introduction

INT. DR. POLLIDORI'S OFFICE—NIGHT

Dr. Pollidori turns back to the monitor, on which is now a grotesque blow up
of a fruit fly head.

> ### DR. POLLIDORI
> Behold Proboscopedia.
>
> ### MULDER
> (looks closer, amazed)
> This fly has legs...
>
> ### SCULLY
> ...growing out of its mouth.
>
> ### MULDER
> (disturbed)
> Why would you want to do that?
>
> ### DR. POLLIDORI
> Because I can.
>
> —"The Post-Modern Prometheus"

A few years ago, I told Chris Carter about a mutant monster every bit as frightening as anything on *The X-Files*. I described its bulging red eyes, spindly neck, and hairy chest that sported three pairs of legs and a pair of wings. A yawn fest, you are thinking? Well, what about an extra pair of legs attached to its forehead or, better yet, coming out of its mouth? And best of all, this monster is no fabrication of a slightly deranged mind. This monster is very real.

Picture the following scene: FBI agent Fox Mulder is relaxing on the couch in his apartment munching on sunflower seeds. A large open window relieves the heat of a midsummer's day. Suddenly, the mutant monster flies in toward the couch, legs flailing from its mouth. Does Mulder jump up and run terrified from the room? On the contrary, the manly Mulder stands and fights. Grabbing the nearest weapon, he whacks at the mutant monstrosity with a fly swatter, killing it on the spot. Um . . . did I forget to mention that this real-life monster is only an eighth of an inch long?

Knowing this last little tidbit, most scriptwriters, even friends, would have smiled lightly while pointing toward the door. To my delight, Chris's eyes lit up. Finally, after years of earnest suggestions, I had come up with something that had sparked his interest.

My acquaintance with this tiny mutant monster began during my first week of graduate school at Indiana University. Dr. Thomas Kaufman from the biology department showed a series of slides that featured the most bizarre creatures I had ever seen. They were fruit flies with wonderful names like *Antennapedia*, the fly with legs where antenna should be, and *Proboscipedia*, the fly with legs coming out of its mouth. As a science fiction fan (then and now) I remember thinking that studying genetics was going to be very interesting.

After telling Chris Carter about the bizarre flies, he paid a visit to Indiana University and spent the day with Tom Kaufman and his laboratory of devoted *X-Files* fans (Kaufman included). Chris returned to Los Angeles with a film loop of a developing fly embryo, a scanning electron microscope picture of *Proboscipedia*, a diagram drawn by Kaufman explaining his science, and a T-shirt from a recent scientific meeting. Using his newly acquired knowledge and souvenirs, Chris wrote one of my favorite *X-Files* episodes: "The Post-Modern Prometheus." In a takeoff on the early Frankenstein movies, Chris invented a "mad scientist" who tinkered with the genes of fruit flies as a springboard to playing with the genomes of people. Chris implied in the episode that the fruit fly *Proboscipedia* was the product of genetic engineering. However, the real origin of *Proboscipedia* didn't involve the intervention of man. This weird mutant owed its deformity to random mutations. Because of a single defective gene, flies were born with legs coming out of their mouths.

Welcome to the wonderful world of genetics. A world where thousands of mutations can have absolutely no effect on an organism while one mutation in the wrong place can produce a monster. Mutations are random, accidental changes to the order of nucleotides in the DNA of a cell. Recall that there are four different kinds of nucleotide beads on a DNA chain. In regions of the DNA that are genes, the order of the four different nucleotides determines the order of amino acids in a protein. Change the succession of nucleotides in a gene and you can change the appearance and function of the protein that it specifies. Mutations can be as simple as a single nucleotide changing to one of the other three or as substantial as the loss or duplication of a large section of DNA. If an important protein gets altered because of a mutation in the DNA, flies can be born with legs dangling from their foreheads.

Can random, individual mutations cause legs to suddenly sprout from your head or turn you into a teenage mutant ninja turtle? Hardly. If a mutation occurs in one of your skin cells, maybe that cell will turn turtle green, but who cares? There are millions of normal skin cells nearby. The only mutations you have to worry about for your own health are ones that disrupt the ability of a cell to remain a good citizen of the body. If mutations transform a liver cell into a cancer cell, then that cell becomes a rogue criminal that no longer cares about the surrounding cells. The mutant cell begins to divide nonstop, producing other cells in its image that also incessantly divide. The gang of mutant cells crowds out normal cells and eventually becomes a tumor.

Mutations can sneak into DNA every time a cell splits in two because the cell must first duplicate its DNA. Once duplicated, the DNA is divided up so that both daughter cells receive the same amount of DNA as was originally found in the parent cell. The process of duplicating DNA is nearly, but not quite, perfect. Polymerases, the enzymes that copy DNA, have the Herculean task of making a perfect replica of DNA chains that contain millions of nucleotide beads. Every time an overworked polymerase makes a mistake and messes up the order of nucleotides without correcting its mistake, a new mutation appears in the DNA of that cell. The imperfection then becomes a permanent part of the cell's genome.

Random mutations in your egg or sperm cells won't affect you but might affect your children. This is because all 100 trillion cells of a child that develop from the mutant egg or sperm will have the mutation—a very different situation from a single cell in your body acquiring the same mutation. Even when they're found in every cell, however, most mutations are still inconsequential. To understand why, imagine that you are duplicating a mostly black drawing on a pretty good copy machine. The duplicated image is nearly, but not quite, identical to the original. Any imperfections, even large ones, which occur in black regions of the drawing won't be noticed. Only tiny specks that stand out against the white background will be visible.

Mutations in DNA are like the imperfections in the copy of a drawing. How consequential a new mutation is depends on its location in the DNA of the genome. Mutations in the 95 percent of the genome that is unused, "junk" DNA (the "black" region of the drawing) will scarcely be noticed. Mutations in the 5 percent of the genome that contains genes have a chance of affecting the organism. Yet even if a mutation in a gene is severe enough to produce a substantially altered protein, the effect on the cell can still be minimal if that particular protein isn't very important or if another protein can take its place.

And then there are the very important proteins—proteins that are the generals of the cell and without which cells can't function normally. When egg or sperm cells acquire mutations in genes that specify important proteins, severe birth defects can result. Some of these important genes are responsible for letting the cells of a developing organism keep track of which parts of the body are which. In the fruit fly, a gene called *Antennapedia* causes the cells near the top of the head to proclaim to other cells, "We're the top of the head!" The chemical message is picked up by proteins on the surfaces of nearby cells, causing antenna to grow in the proper place. Mess up the *Antennapedia* gene, and the cells near the top of the head incorrectly cry out, "We're the thorax, stupid, make some legs!" So legs appear where antenna should be. Humans also have the same important genes that lay out the segments of the body. Unlike flies, which can live quite happily with legs flopping from their heads, such mutations in humans only lead to live births on *The X-Files*.

If your only knowledge of mutations and mutants comes from comic books or television, you might think that most mutations are beneficial to an organism. Mutations in the media turn dumb turtles into wisecracking, crime-fighting, pizza-loving heroes, or give amazing, superhuman mental and physical powers to ordinary people who like to wear colorful skintight clothing. In truth, if you consider only mutations that have some effect on an organism, the vast majority of mutations are detrimental. Mutations tend to be harmful because it's easier to mess up a protein than improve it. If you put a gaggle of five-year-olds together with hammers and new television sets in a room and tell each child to give a TV a whack, chances are that reception will not improve. In the same way, just about every mutation will have either no effect on a protein or will make it worse. Protein function is rarely improved by random mutations.

This is the seeming paradox of evolution. Mutations are required to drive the evolution of an organism yet nearly all mutations are inconsequential or detrimental. Evolution, though, is not a paradox if you think of it as a force that is acting on a large population over a very long time. Somewhere, sometime, out of the millions of hammer-wielding five-year-olds, one will whack a TV and make it work better. Engineers will take it apart (the TV, not the kid), figure out what went right, and TVs all over the world will be produced in its image. Evolution has had millions of years to respond to the occasional beneficial mutation. A mutation that results in a better immune system would keep an individual alive in a world beset by pathogens. That person would be in a better position to pass on her genes to the next generation as others less fortunate perish from disease.

Even today, examples can be found of rare beneficial mutant genes that are driving evolution. As HIV continues to cause AIDS and death for large numbers of people worldwide, some individuals who are at high risk never become infected with the virus. Is it good fortune, or is there something in their genome? Scientists looking for connections among these lucky people found one. A mutant gene that helps protect people from HIV is found in the genomes of 10 percent of people descended from Northern Europeans. If two copies of the defective gene are present, as they are in 1 percent of this population, then these fortunate people are able to resist becoming infected with HIV. The mutation is in the gene for a protein that normally hangs out on the surface of immune cells and provides a doorway for the invasion of the virus. If this protein is damaged or not present, the virus has a very difficult time entering and infecting cells. This faulty but beneficial gene is not found in South Americans, Africans, or Asians.

So why, you might ask, are Northern Europeans so fortunate? Good fortune today may have come at the expense of a terrible catastrophe many years ago. For a mutant gene to become widespread in a limited population, something must have occurred where a person's very survival was dependent on having the mutation. Since infection by HIV was unheard of twenty years ago, that "something" was likely a different epidemic. With a reasonable estimate of the frequency with which one population produces another, and a pretty powerful computer, some scientists have calculated the date when the mutant gene was probably first present in more than just a few people. That date is approximately seven hundred years ago, the time when the bubonic plague was sweeping through Northern Europe, decimating the population. Bubonic plague, like HIV, is a disease of the immune system. Survivors of the plague either lived in isolated villages or had a mutant gene that conferred immunity to the plague bacterium. If the mutant gene was present in 1 percent of the population before the epidemic, it may have been found in 90 percent of the vastly reduced population after the plague killed off the people who did not have the gene. Some scientists believe that this same gene protects the descendants of plague survivors from HIV.

Another example of a beneficial mutation is a defect in the gene for hemoglobin. The hemoglobin protein is responsible for carrying oxygen from each breath to the cells of the body. Everyone has two copies of the hemoglobin gene. If only one copy is faulty, there are few consequences to the individual—the remaining good copy specifies enough protein to transport sufficient amounts of oxygen. If both copies are faulty, the person has a potentially life-threatening disease called sickle-cell anemia. About 10 percent of adults of African heritage have one good and one faulty version of the hemoglobin gene.

The benefit derived from having one defective version of the hemoglobin gene is now known. It protects against malaria. Malaria is a terrible disease caused by *Plasmodium,* a single-cell parasite that is transmitted to people by mosquitoes. Three hundred million people a year, mostly in Africa, are afflicted with malaria, leading to 2.7 million annual deaths. If you have one good and one bad version of the hemoglobin gene, you are much less likely to get malaria. It is not hard to imagine a time before modern medicine and mosquito control programs when an even larger percentage of the African population died each year from malaria. Those fortunate enough to have one bad version of the hemoglobin gene didn't get malaria and so lived longer than less fortunate people who had only "normal" hemoglobin. In the past, the benefits to an individual who had the mutant gene far outweighed the low chances that a child would inherit two bad versions of the gene and die from sickle-cell anemia. This is hardly a comfort to many African Americans who no longer derive any benefit from being protected against malaria yet have to experience the heartbreak of children with sickle-cell anemia.

Epidemics such as malaria and bubonic plague are cited by some as evidence that evolution doesn't proceed at a slow and steady pace. Such diseases, or equally calamitous geological upheavals, could cause isolated pockets of people or other organisms to evolve more rapidly than their less stressed brethren. The new and improved species might coexist today with the original species or might have grinded the parental species into the dust. Such sudden changes, found in the fossil record, followed by relative stasis, is called punctuated equilibrium by Niles Eldredge and Stephen J. Gould. Devotees of *The X-Files* may recall Mulder referring to this theory in the episode "Leonard Betts."

In the realm of science fiction, mutations frequently lead to the generation of monsters. While most science fiction monsters tend to be fearsome mutant animals with a curious need to destroy New York or Tokyo, the monsters in *The X-Files* are mainly human. There is the Peacock family, whose monstrous exteriors hide a dark family secret; Victor, a translator of ancient Italian who brings new meaning to the term "high fat diet"; Leonard Betts, the mild-mannered emergency medical technician who doesn't mind losing his head if the situation demands it; and a janitor who is every woman's dream date. These human monsters provoke fear in viewers, but also sympathy. They did not choose their violent natures, they were born that way. The peculiar appetites and behaviors of *X-Files'* mutants are the unhappy consequences of defective genes. Although *X-Files* monsters kill, they take no pleasure in it. Killing is a means to survive—to eat, or to hide their mutancy from others who would destroy them.

When Mulder asks Dr. Polidori, the fictional Dr. Frankenstein–like scientist in "The Post-Modern Prometheus," why he created flies with legs coming out of their mouths, Polidori replies, "Because I can." After Chris's visit to Indiana University, he phoned to ask why Dr. Kaufman was studying those flies. I responded that understanding why flies become severely handicapped due to a single defective gene can help scientists learn how some genes control the fates of many different genes. By studying these types of mutants, scientists are uncovering the secrets of genetics and development. In "The Post-Modern Prometheus," Mulder asks Scully why Dr. Polidori is doing these experiments. Scully replies, "To unlock the mysteries of genetics—to understand how it is that even though we share the same genes, we develop arms instead of wings—we become humans instead of flies or monsters." I couldn't have said it better myself.

Genes 'R Us

In nearly every town, there is a place that can only be described as eerie. Perhaps it is the location of a dilapidated structure where no one ever seems to go in or out, or a yard where only the bravest of children will venture to retrieve an errant projectile. The Peacock property in the episode "Home" is such a place. When the audience first peers inside, a tortured woman is giving birth under barbaric conditions. As lightning flashes in the night sky, a horribly disfigured baby is born. The three shambling men that witness the birth pick up the crying newborn and bury it alive in a nearby field. Children playing baseball accidentally unearth the dead infant, whose appearance is so inhuman that the sheriff summons Mulder and Scully to the scene. Scully takes one look at the baby and is aghast to find that it suffered from multiple rare birth defects including Neu-Laxova syndrome, Meckel-Gruber syndrome, and extrophy of cloaca.

Scully's knowledge of medical genetics is vast indeed to have recognized the symptoms of these very real disorders since there are so few reported cases of Neu-Laxova syndrome or Meckel-Gruber syndrome. Perhaps Scully had recently studied the book *Smith's Recognizable Patterns of Human Malformation*, which summarizes a large number of human deformities. In an astonishing coincidence, two of Baby Peacock's rare abnormalities are featured back-to-back on pages 152 and 153 in this well-known compilation of human afflictions.

Neu-Laxova syndrome is extremely rare and always fatal. Scully must have noticed the small head with a sloped forehead, small protruding eyes, gaping mouth, and lack of chin or any hair. If the baby hadn't suffocated from being buried alive, it would have lived only briefly because of the massive central nervous system damage and incomplete brain. Meckel-Gruber syndrome is slightly more common, but just as fatal. Scully probably based her diagnosis on seeing the brain protruding from the skull, the short neck and extra digits associated with this heartbreaking syndrome.

Neu-Laxova syndrome and Meckel-Gruber syndrome are two of more than four thousand genetic diseases identified to date. For a disorder to have a genetic basis, the DNA of one or more genes must be different from normal. Genetic diseases are rarely the products of new mutations. Rather, they are the consequences of mutations in genes that occurred long ago—legacies from ancestors long dead.

More specifically, genetic diseases and immunities, and much else, are gifts from your parents. People inherit 3 billion nucleotides from Mom and another 3 billion from Dad. Join the 6 billion nucleotides of the human genome from end to end and the chain would reach over three feet . . . and it all has to fit into the nucleus of a human cell two hundred times smaller than the period at the end of this sentence. It helps that the human genome is not one massive chain of DNA but is divided into 46 pieces called chromosomes.

Chromosomes come in large and small sizes, depending on the length of their DNA chain. If you look into the nucleus of one of your cells, the DNA would appear long and stringy, much like a plate of spaghetti. Distinguishing individual chromosomes among the forty-six residents of the nuclear soup is like trying to trace a single spaghetti strand in a heaping helping, especially when covered with tangy cellular meat sauce. Analyzing chromosomes is easier when a cell gets ready to divide. At that time, each chromosome's DNA chain vastly condenses in size, making a chromosome look more like an individual sausage. Chromosomes at their most condensed can be easily seen with the help of a light microscope.

Getting a two-inch-long chain of DNA to fit into the tiny dimensions of a supercondensed chromosome is like trying to stuff a rubber band the length of a football field into the football. If you and a partner hold a 100-yard-long rubber band at either end and begin twisting it, the rubber band starts shrinking as it coils into a neat spiral pattern. As you keep twisting, the coils twist on top of previous coils, and the rubber band shrinks further and further in size. Finally, the coils are so compact that the rubber band condenses into a small object, about the size of a football. The compacting of DNA into a chromosome is a bit more organized, but it is essentially the same idea.

Scully sends away some of Baby Peacock's tissue to the FBI lab so that the infant's chromosomes can be examined. When Scully holds up the completed chart of the baby's chromosomes, you can see the supercompacted chromosomes from a cell that was moments away from splitting into two cells. Chromosomes in this compacted form look like Siamese twin sausages, connected somewhere along the length. The sausages are "twins" because the DNA has been duplicated, which occurs right before a cell is ready to divide. The DNA chains of all forty-six chromosome sausages must be duplicated so that a copy of each chromosome ends up in each of the two daughter cells. As the cell divides, the Siamese twin sausages break apart with one sausage ending up in one cell and the other ending up in the sister cell. This division of Siamese twin sausages into the two daughter cells occurs for all forty-six chromosomes each time a cell divides. The result is that every new cell has precisely the same number of chromosomes as the parent cell.

Chromosomes come in two varieties, known as autosomes and sex chromosomes. You have twenty-two different autosomes, numbered from 1 to 22 according to their size. Autosomes always come in pairs, so in every cell there are two chromosome 1's, two chromosome 2's, and so on. Along with your twenty-two pairs of autosomal chromosomes, you have two sex chromosomes. If you are a woman, you have two X chromosomes; if you are a man, you have one X and one Y chromosome. Twenty-three of your forty-six chromosomes were inherited from your mother and the remaining twenty-three came from your father. Each of your parents provided you with one of every autosome and one of your two sex chromosomes.

If you open up one of your almost-ready-to-divide cells and scatter your chromosomes on a piece of glass, you would see forty-six chromosomes of various sizes if you use a light microscope. The two largest chromosomes, which look like Siamese twin sausages connected in mid-length, are easy to spot. Those would be your two chromosome 1's. At the other end of the spectrum, you would see two tiny chromosomes connected near one end—those are your chromosome 22's. The sizes of your other chromosomes are somewhere between these two extremes. Some chromosomes are so similar in size and appearance that it is impossible to tell them apart without help. Determining which of your scattered chromosomes are number 9's and which are number 10's, for example, requires special treatment of the DNA so that a particular chromosome will fluoresce with a unique color.

The chart displaying Baby Peacock's chromosomes in the episode is typical of a chromosome chart. To produce this type of chart, a digital image is taken of color-treated chromosomes from a single busted cell by a camera hooked up to a microscope. With the help of a computer (which replaces the scissors and adhesive tape I used when playing with Polaroid pictures of chromosomes in college), chromosomes are "cut" and "pasted" for placement in pairs from 1 to 22. The two sex chromosomes are always last on the chart, either two X chromosomes together or one X paired up with the much smaller Y chromosome. The most frequent need to open up a cell and lay out the chromosomes on a chart is when couples want to know the sex of their baby before birth. If the baby's two sex chromosomes are X's, it is a girl; X and Y, and it's a boy. Two Y chromosomes, and it's an alien.

Scully wants to examine a chart of Baby Peacock's chromosomes since severe deformities in babies can sometimes be traced to visible changes in chromosomes. Many genetic diseases occur because a chromosome has lost a large chunk of DNA from one or both ends of the chain—DNA that contained important genes. Recall that a gene is simply a short region along the DNA chain that gets copied into the similar molecule, RNA, which is then used as an instruction sheet for making a protein. All proteins have a job to do, with some jobs being more critical than others. If a chromosome is missing a piece of DNA so large that the chromosome is visibly shorter than normal, then a number of genes will also be missing. When Scully analyzes Baby Peacock's chromosomes, she mentions that there is noticeable chromosomal breakage, meaning that whole segments of DNA chains have broken off and are missing.

Scully refers to Neu-Laxova syndrome and Meckel-Gruber syndrome as "autosomal dominant disorders." Scully doesn't explain this statement since it would have taken her the remainder of the episode. While "Home" is one of my favorite *X-Files*, some viewers may have preferred a lengthy soliloquy on genetics to learning the dark and disturbing secret of the Peacock clan.

Scully is correct when she tells Mulder that Neu-Laxova and Meckel-Gruber syndromes are autosomal diseases. This means that the defective genes resulting in these syndromes are located somewhere on autosomes and not on sex chromosomes. Scully doesn't say which autosomes contain the faulty genes because that information isn't known. Simply knowing that the disease genes are autosomal is like being told that San Antonio and Los Angeles are cities in the United States and not Mexico, only you aren't told which states the cities are in or how close the cities are to each other. Just a few thousand of the 100,000 human genes have had their precise positions on the chromosome "map" determined so far. Once the Human Genome Project is completed, scientists will be able to determine the precise locations of defective genes that cause rare genetic diseases like Neu-Laxova and Meckel-Gruber syndromes. It's important to keep in mind, though, that just knowing where a disease-causing gene happens to be on a chromosome doesn't mean that a cure is in sight. Knowing that Los Angeles is in California tells you nothing about the population, the weather, the schools, or whether it's a nice place to vacation. It only tells you where it's located.

When Scully explains to Mulder that Neu-Laxova and Meckel-Gruber syndromes are "dominant" genetic disorders, she is referring to the relationship between different versions of a gene. Since everyone has two of each autosomal chromosome, everyone has two versions of every gene found on an autosome. The two versions of any gene can be either identical to each other or different from each other. Let's consider the gene that determines the shape of your earlobes. Some people, like me, have loose earlobes. Other people, like my husband, have attached earlobes and consequently can't wear quite as many earrings. The gene that determines earlobe shape is located on an autosome so everyone has two versions of the earlobe gene. These versions can specify attached earlobes or loose earlobes. If you have two attached versions of the earlobe gene, you have attached earlobes; if you have two loose versions, you have loose earlobes. But what if you have one loose version and one attached version? For earlobe shape, the loose version of the gene is the more important one. It dominates the attached version. Versions of genes that dominate other versions are called *dominant*. The meek versions of genes are called *recessive*. This means that if you have one loose version and one attached version of the earlobe gene, you will have loose earlobes. Look in the mirror. If you have attached earlobes, you must have two attached versions of the earlobe gene.

This hierarchy of gene versions is common. Take hair color. If you have a brown version and a blond version, you will have brown hair. Brown is dominant to blond. Anyone who has blond hair either has two blond versions of the gene or makes regular visits to a hairdresser. Mr. Spock of the starship *Enterprise,* half human and half Vulcan, has pointed ears. This means that the pointed-ear version of the gene he inherited from his Vulcan father is dominant to the round-ear version of the gene he inherited from his human mother. When Scully calls Neu-Laxova and Meckel-Gruber syndromes "dominant disorders," she means that the defective version of the Neu-Laxova syndrome gene dominates the normal version of the gene. Having one defective version of any dominant disorder is enough to give someone the disease. It doesn't matter if you also have a normal version of the gene.

This is the story behind Huntington's disease, an autosomal dominant genetic disease that devastates the lives of about one in every ten thousand people. Everyone afflicted with Huntington's disease has a normal version of the gene on one of their chromosome 4's and a defective version on the other chromosome 4 that specifies a faulty protein that clumps when it shouldn't. Since parents contribute one of each of their autosomes to their children, a mother with Huntington's can contribute either her normal chromosome 4 or her disease-bearing chromosome 4 to her child. This means that there is a fifty-fifty chance of passing on the chromosome containing the defective gene to each child. The degeneration of neurons associated with Huntington's doesn't begin until a person reaches her thirties or forties, so whether or not one has inherited the faulty gene from an afflicted parent usually isn't known before having one's own children and possibly passing the defective gene on to them. Genetic testing is now available for people with a sick parent, but most choose to remain ignorant of their genetic fate.

If Scully is correct, and Neu-Laxova and Meckel-Gruber syndromes are dominant autosomal disorders like Huntington's, then Baby Peacock's father or mother must have had the defective genes. If the father or mother has the same lethal syndromes as Baby Peacock, and these syndromes are dominant, he or she would have been, ah, dead at birth. Is this another X-File?

Actually, the answer is more mundane. Scully, no doubt dismayed at the sight of poor Baby Peacock, makes a slight error when talking about the syndromes. They are in reality not autosomal *dominant* disorders but rather autosomal *recessive* disorders. To be afflicted with an autosomal recessive disorder, you need both versions of a particular gene to be faulty. If you inherit only one faulty version of a gene, you don't have the disease. Your normal version of the gene dominates the defective version. You are, however, considered to be a carrier of the disease. This means that you can pass on the defective version of the gene to your offspring. If you are fortunate and marry someone who doesn't have a defective version of the same gene, your children cannot inherit the disease. They can only become carriers like yourself. If you are unfortunate and marry someone who is also a carrier of the same disease, your children have a one in four chance of inheriting both your bad copy of the gene and your spouse's.

This is the genetic roulette of cystic fibrosis and other autosomal recessive disorders. Cystic fibrosis is caused by a tiny flaw in a gene on chromosome 7. This gene specifies a protein that normally makes tunnels through plasma membranes, the coverings that surround all cells. These particular tunnels are for the exclusive use by the chemical chloride, so that chloride can vacate the cell when necessary. A flaw in the gene for the tunnel protein means that the tunnel is either not made or it's defective. This seemingly innocuous transportation problem of a single chemical leads to respiratory and digestive problems that take an enormous toll on the health of the afflicted individual.

If a room contains twenty-one Caucasians, chances are that one of them is a carrier of the cystic fibrosis gene and doesn't know it. After all, that person will never show any signs of the disease. In the past, it was beneficial to have one faulty version of the cystic fibrosis gene since it may have offered protection against typhoid fever—hardly a comfort in the United States today. As long as a carrier of the cystic fibrosis gene marries someone with two normal versions of the cystic fibrosis gene, there is no chance that any of their children will have the disease, since the children will always inherit at least one normal version of the gene. But mates are chosen for reasons other than invisible genes. About one in every two thousand children born in the United States has cystic fibrosis. For most parents, the devastating diagnosis of their child is the first inkling that they are both carriers of the faulty gene.

Baby Peacock's problems go far beyond the autosomal recessive diseases of Neu-Laxova and Meckel-Gruber syndromes. Observant viewers of Baby Peacock's chromosome chart probably noticed that there are far more than the normal 46 chromosomes. Baby Peacock has 92 chromosomes—four copies of each chromosome instead of the normal two! When it comes to chromosomes, more is definitely not better. Millions of years of evolution have led to precisely the correct number and types of genes to form a living, breathing, usually rational person. Extra copies of genes are not good. It's like throwing an extra valve into a precision sports car without retooling the rest of the engine. Instead of getting a more powerful car, the result is a defective lemon.

Having even one extra chromosome can lead to very severe birth defects, when it permits the fetus to survive at all. Down's syndrome, a duplication of tiny chromosome 21, occurs in about one out of every one thousand births. Instead of the normal two copies of chromosome 21, people with Down's syndrome have three copies. Only two other autosomal chromosomes, numbers 13 and 18, can be duplicated and still lead to live births. Unfortunately, the severe physical problems associated with having extra versions of the genes found on these two chromosomes mean that survival is rare beyond the first year.

While extra autosomal chromosomes are normally a death sentence, extra sex chromosomes are not. There is already an unequal number of X chromosomes between men and women. Women have twice as many X chromosomes as men, yet survive the experience quite nicely. On the contrary, having only a single X chromosome is not always in the best interest of men. By having only a single version of every gene on the X chromosome, men are more likely than women to have genetic diseases that involve faulty X chromosome genes. The best-known genetic disease connected with the X chromosome is hemophilia. For women to have the disease, both of their X chromosomes need to have the faulty version of the gene. Men, however, have only a single X chromosome, which they inherit from Mom. If that single X chromosome has the defective gene, the son will have hemophilia. The gene for color blindness is also located on the X chromosome, which is why so many men and so few women are color-blind.

Scientists used to puzzle over how finely tuned human cells could function regardless of whether they contain one or two X chromosomes. The answer came in the mid part of the twentieth century when it was discovered that a random X chromosome in every woman's cells curls up into a little ball and becomes dormant. Most of the genes on the inactive X chromosome no longer function so that just like men's cells, women's cells have only one active X chromosome. This natural process, called X-chromosome inactivation, is the reason why having extra copies of the X chromosome is not a death sentence. Women can live with several extra copies of the X chromosome, since all but one would be inactivated in each cell.

X-chromosome inactivation is the secret behind beautifully colored calico cats. Ever wonder why all calico cats are female? The cat gene for black and orange hair color is on the X chromosome. Since male cats have only one X chromosome, they can have either the black version of the gene, and be black, or the orange version of the gene, and be orange, but they can't be both colors at the same time. A female cat can have both a black version and an orange version of the color gene on her two X chromosomes. During kitty embryo development, patches of black and orange color appear because in every one of her cells, only one X chromosome actually functions. If the chromosome containing the black version is inactivated in one cell, then the cell will produce an orange color due to the orange version on the remaining active X chromosome. All the cells derived from that cell have the same X chromosome inactivated. You can tell from the sizes and locations of the color patches on the female cat which cells are the direct descendants of a cell that first inactivated one of its X chromosomes.

If Baby Peacock's only problem was an extra X chromosome, it would have few obvious physical manifestations besides being taller and thinner than average. Baby Peacock's genetic problems are severe, however, by virtue of having two entire extra sets of chromosomes. Scully is so shocked to see all the extra chromosomes on the chart that she first concludes that someone in the lab must have botched the test. Babies rarely develop with one extra set of chromosomes so it is a miracle that Baby Peacock survived long enough to be born with two extra sets. Realizing that the chromosome chart is most likely accurate, Scully and Mulder propose separate theories for how Baby Peacock ended up with so many extra chromosomes.

Scully's theory for the extra two sets of chromosomes is a "maldivision of the centromere." The more correct scientific term for what Scully is referring to is "chromosomal nondisjunction." I'm glad that I was able to clear that up. However, for those of you who don't dust around your genetics degree every week, here's what Scully is talking about. All of us begin as a single cell, the fusion of egg and sperm sex cells. To generate these sex cells, cells called germ cells must go through the type of cell division called meiosis. During meiosis, daughter cells are produced that contain precisely half of the chromosomes—one of each autosome and one of the two sex chromosomes—of the original germ cell. That way, when the twenty-three chromosomes in the egg cell and the twenty-three chromosomes in the sperm cell come together during fertilization, a never before and never again in the history of man concoction of forty-six chromosomes join forces to create a new and unique person . . . like you.

Two out of every one hundred pregnancies start with a fertilized egg that mistakenly has three sets of chromosomes instead of the normal two. Scully's theory is that Baby Peacock has two extra sets of chromosomes because of a problem that occurred when a germ cell was dividing into two daughter sex cells. In some embryos that have an entire extra set of chromosomes, one of the original germ cells didn't divide into two daughter cells like it was supposed to. Only one daughter sex cell was produced, with all forty-six chromosomes instead of the normal twenty-three. Fuse this sex cell (say, it's an egg) with a normal sperm cell and the fertilized egg will have three complete sets of chromosomes—forty-six from the egg and twenty-three from the sperm. If both egg and sperm have an extra set of chromosomes, the fertilized egg will have two extra sets, which is Scully's explanation for what happened to Baby Peacock.

Mulder has a different theory. He believes that more than one sperm fertilized the egg. Although eggs have developed mechanisms to prevent fertilization by multiple sperm, these mechanisms are not always successful. Two thirds of the time when an embryo has three sets of chromosomes, the extra set is due to fertilization by two sperm. Otherwise, extra sets of chromosomes are due to mistakes in meiosis—Scully's theory. So the odds are that Mulder is correct.

Baby Peacock is the poster child for genetic disorders. The probability of so many genetic problems appearing in one child is virtually zero unless the family ignored religious and state laws and practiced inbreeding—the mating of couples who are closely related to each other. There are good reasons why laws exist against inbreeding. If your genome is similar to the average, you are a carrier of five to ten lethal recessive versions of different genes and a host of versions of other defective recessive genes that are incapacitating but not lethal. This isn't something to worry about for your own health since the normal version of each gene dominates over the disease version. The chances are also small that you will marry someone who also has one of the same defective gene versions, which is the only way that your children could inherit two versions of a disease gene and have the disease. This is not the case for a population where inbreeding is common. The more related people are to each other, the more similar is their genetic makeup, and the more likely that two bad versions of the same gene end up in the children.

Inbred human populations, usually involving marriage between cousins, are not an uncommon phenomenon. On nineteenth-century Martha's Vineyard, an island off the coast of Massachusetts, the town of Chilmark was a half day's journey from any other village. As a result, residents of Chilmark intermarried, which brought out a genetic type of deafness. More than one quarter of Chilmark's residents were deaf and everyone in town could converse in sign language. Chilmark is no longer isolated so incidences of deafness are now rare. Inbreeding can also occur when groups become culturally isolated, marrying only members of the same small religious, political, or ethnic group. This has happened with the Amish and Mennonite communities of North America, who suffer from a rare form of short-limbed dwarfism, and the Choctaw Indians of Oklahoma, who have a high prevalence of systemic sclerosis, a disease of the skin and internal organs.

The sheriff tells Mulder and Scully that the Peacock family have a long tradition of inbreeding. The Peacock brothers, however, were in a quandary since the last related woman, their mother, was thought to have died in a car accident ten years back. This information leads Mulder and Scully to suggest that the boys kidnapped a traveler to be the mother of the next generation of Peacock babies. Such a scenario would be unlikely, though, since some of Baby Peacock's disorders were recessive. The random abductee also would have to be a carrier of the same very rare disorders as her captors. The dark truth is revealed soon afterward. The mother of the Peacock boys survived the car accident. The older brother is both father and brother of the younger Peacock boys, and at least one of the brothers was the father of Baby Peacock.

Scully's original diagnosis of Baby Peacock's problems included the uncommon disorder "extrophy of cloaca." Extrophy of cloaca actually isn't a genetic disorder, but a nonfatal mistake in the early development of the fetus that leads to a series of lower abdominal deformities. Many children are born with birth defects unrelated to defective genes. For example, children of mothers that smoke during pregnancy can have low birth weights, respiratory problems, and mental retardation, none of which are caused by faults in the child's DNA.

"You are what you eat" is a common axiom, but while you were in the womb, you were what your mom was eating. The most notorious example of a chemical eaten by pregnant mothers that led to deformed babies was the drug thalidomide. Thalidomide was produced by the Chemie Grunenthal pharmaceutical company in West Germany in 1957. In forty-six countries, thalidomide was marketed as a nontoxic wonder drug—no side effects, no morning sickness, and a safe night's sleep for pregnant women. Insomnia turned out to be only one of the side effects of taking the drug. Chemie Grunenthal had tested thalidomide on animals, but in an astonishing omission by today's standards, the company never bothered to test the drug on pregnant animals. The extent of the thalidomide disaster was soon apparent. As many as twelve thousand babies were born without arms or legs or both. Scientists estimate that for every child who survived to birth, three more died in the womb.

There are probably thousands of baby boomers in the United States who owe their physical health or even their lives to Dr. Frances Kelsey, a scientist who works for the United States Food and Drug Administration (FDA). In one of the great early triumphs of the FDA, thalidomide was never approved for use in America. Dr. Kelsey was given thalidomide as her first drug approval decision because it should have been a simple vote of yes. After all, the drug was being used in Canada and all over the world. Dr. Kelsey aggressively fought a one-woman crusade against the approval of thalidomide. The pharmaceutical company could not answer her questions on how the drug worked, and without that information, Dr. Kelsey thought that thalidomide was potentially too dangerous for distribution. It wasn't until 1961 that a link was made between as little as a single dose of thalidomide and birth defects. When tests of the drug were finally conducted on pregnant animals, the same types of rare birth defects were found. It is now known that thalidomide works by stopping the development of blood vessels, which guide the growth of limbs and organs. Thalidomide is still used in some countries to successfully treat leprosy, certain types of cancer, and AIDS. The FDA has recently approved the use of thalidomide in the United States for the treatment of leprosy, but only under highly restrictive conditions.

It is not clear why the Peacock baby suffered from nongenetic as well as genetic disorders. Lack of prenatal care, poor nutrition, and the unsanitary conditions in the house may all have played a role in the nongenetic birth defects. The genetic disorders were clearly the consequences of years of inbreeding and the inheritance of multiple lethal versions of genes. The laws of genetics were also not kind to the three Peacock boys. One brother has no scalp hair, another has patchy hair. All seem to have some overgrowth of facial bones, and walk with stooped posture and shambling gaits. None of them speak and they don't seem to feel any pain. After a final showdown with Mulder and Scully, only one brother and the mother remain alive. Before Mulder and Scully can stop them, mother and son drive off looking for a new home where they can continue passing on the Peacock genes.

Like Father, Like Son

According to the supermarket tabloids, aliens have been living among us for quite some time. Walk past most checkout counters and headlines such as SPACE ALIEN ATE MY CHILD, ADMITS PROCTOLOGIST, UFO FOUND ON JUPITER!—SHOCKING TAPES REVEALED, and ALIENS FROM PLUTO LANDED IN MY LIVING ROOM AND TORTURED THIRTY-NINE BANANAS vie for your attention. Only people who see aliens behind every unusual phenomenon could possibly take these stories seriously.

In the *X-Files* episode "Small Potatoes," Mulder drags a reluctant Scully to West Virginia to investigate the tabloid headline *Monkey Babies Invade Small Town*. The story describes the births of five babies with tails in a five-month period. Scully tells Mulder that a fetus normally develops with a tail but it is usually lost early during fetal development. Five children born with tails in a small town is highly unusual. Although Scully doesn't mention the precise numbers, only about twenty-four babies have been born with tails since 1884. In seven of these cases, the babies could actually wag the tails when crying or coughing, just like the babies in this episode. Since the persistence of tails in babies doesn't seem to have a genetic basis, Scully thinks that the defect in the West Virginia babies is due to a non-genetic disorder. Investigation is warranted, but by the Health Department, not the FBI. Scully suspects that Mulder has more interest in the second part of the headline, *Did West Virginia women mate with visitors from space?*

At the hospital, Mulder and Scully interview the latest mother, who names Luke Skywalker as the father. The mother asks Scully if Luke could also be the father of the other children. Genetic tests of the DNA of her baby and the other four "monkey" babies indicate that one man did indeed father all the children, but not necessarily Luke Skywalker.

The genetic test used in "Small Potatoes" and other *X-Files* episodes to determine parenthood uses a laboratory method called polymerase chain reaction, or PCR. PCR is commonly used to test for parentage since it can determine if a child's DNA is a combination of the DNA of the parents. In criminal investigations, PCR can also be used to match two DNA samples to each other. PCR is simply a method for making copies of a segment of DNA. Millions of copies. Enough copies so that the DNA becomes visible after applying a stain. Imagine that there is a piece of thread on the floor of your room— you probably wouldn't see it. Now imagine a million copies of the thread together on the floor. You couldn't miss them. It's the same with DNA. Before you can analyze two DNA samples to see if there is a match, you need to be able to see them.

It's probably not obvious why being able to see DNA can tell you something about parentage. The key is the choice of DNA sections that are copied. Some regions of DNA tend to vary between people, and these are the regions chosen to be copied in a PCR test. Many such variances in people's DNA are due to different numbers of repetitions of particular nucleotides in "junk" regions of the genome between genes. Consider, for example, the following sentence: THE DOG AND THE THE CAT ATE THE BAT. Each of the letters is like a nucleotide in a DNA chain. There are nine letters between "DOG" and "CAT," since the nucleotide letters T- H- E are repeated twice. Now take another similar sentence: THE DOG AND THE THE THE THE CAT ATE THE BAT. In this sentence, there are 15 letters between "DOG" and "CAT." If you were to make a copy of the segment of the sentence between DOG and CAT, one would obviously be longer than the other. The more repeats of the letters T-H-E, the larger the segment produced. The same is true for segments of DNA.

Scientists have identified a number of regions in the human genome that are different sizes in unrelated people because of different numbers of repetitions of three nucleotides. If you examine the sizes of DNA pieces from several of these regions, a unique profile can be generated for every person. If the PCR test is run on a baby and mother's DNA, the mother's contribution to the baby's DNA profile can be factored out, leaving only the contribution of the unknown father. For the five children born with tails, Scully learns that they all shared an abnormally small PCR fragment on chromosome 8 that the mother did not have. It could only have come from the mysterious father.

Mulder and Scully visit a clinic where four of the five mothers received insemination therapy. When a janitor at the clinic bends over while working, Mulder notices a scar indicative of a removed tail. The janitor immediately replaces Luke Skywalker at the top of the list of father suspects. When it's discovered that the janitor's father also had a tail, a genetic cause for the birth defect becomes more clear. Even Mulder discards his "fathered by an alien" theory in favor of simple human parentage.

Although Scully does not expound on the genetics of the tail trait, there is enough information provided in the episode to determine that the tail is due to an autosomal dominant genetic defect. How do I know this? First, the tail defect must be on an autosomal chromosome and not a sex chromosome because it was passed from father to janitor son and from son to at least one baby daughter. This couldn't happen if the tail gene was on the X or Y sex chromosomes. Fathers pass down their Y chromosome to sons and their X chromosome to daughters. If the trait is on the Y chromosome, only sons could inherit the defect, and the latest baby wagging a tail is a girl. If the defective gene is on the X chromosome, then the father of the janitor could not have passed the chromosome to his son because sons only inherit their father's Y chromosome. The gene therefore has to be on an autosome to be passed down from father to son and from son to daughter (see how handy a Ph.D. in genetics can be?).

The dominant nature of the tail trait can be deduced from the inheritance of the tail in successive generations. If the trait is dominant, then only one bad version of the gene is required to have a tail. If the trait is recessive, then all the mothers must also have the very rare "tail" version of the gene, an unlikely scenario unless inbreeding was rampant in the town. A dominant trait means that the janitor has a fifty-fifty chance of passing down the "tail" gene to his children. Since five children were identified with tails, there were probably more unsuspected offspring of the janitor that did not inherit the tail.

The mothers of the children had no idea that their husbands

were not the true fathers because the janitor could change his appearance and masquerade as other people, including the intrepid Luke Skywalker. An autopsy of the janitor's deceased father indicates that he had an additional muscle that Mulder believes allowed him and his son to morph their appearance and vocal cords. (If you're waiting for a scientific explanation for morphing, you'll be waiting a long time.) Scully wonders if there is a link between the "morphing" gene and the gene that results in a tail. She is not suggesting that these are manifestations of the same defective gene. Rather, gene linkage refers to the location of genes on the chromosome map. If two genes are located near each other on the DNA chain in one chromosome, then they will be inherited together when that particular chromosome ends up in a sex cell. This means that the five babies in the hospital with tails also have inherited the ability to morph their appearance. Given the difficulties of raising a child whose appearance doesn't change, one can only pity what the parents of the small potato babies will be facing in the years to come.

Food, Glorious Food

INT. INTERROGATION ROOM—DAY

                    VIRGIL
You look at this hideous monster...but I was only feeding a
hunger.

                    SCULLY
You're more than a monster. You didn't just prey on their bodies—you preyed on their minds.

                    VIRGIL
My weakness was no greater than theirs. I gave them what
they wanted. They gave me what I needed.

                                        —"2Shy"

A man and a woman, corresponding by means of an impersonal keyboard and screen, decide to take their relationship to the next level and meet in person in the *X-Files* episode "2Shy." A glance at the man and you can understand why at he would want to correspond in a non-visual manner. His skin contains patches of dry scales that a woman interested only in outward appearances might find distasteful. The woman, Lauren, no runway model herself, looks past his exterior because of the beautiful words he communicated to her by modem and now in person. Together in a car, isolated from prying eyes, they meet, they kiss, and a beautiful new relationship blossoms. . . . Of course if that's what really happened, *The X-Files* would hardly have lasted into its seventh season. So back up. They meet, they kiss . . . and a thick, gooey liquid spews from his mouth into hers. Lauren struggles to break the kiss as the slobbery substance burns her insides like acid. The man continues to hold their lips together as he sucks out her jellified innards. Now, that's romance on *The X-Files*.

By the time Mulder and Scully arrive on the scene, Lauren's body is nearly completely dissolved. Only a thin layer of goo surrounds her brittle skeleton. Scully analyzes some of the material responsible for Lauren's meltdown and discovers that the slime is mostly organic with a high content of hydrochloric acid. She tells Mulder that the material is similar to that secreted by the gastric mucosa, only somewhat more acidic. Scully also finds traces of pepsin, which she describes as a digestive enzyme.

Scully makes a slight mistake when referring to the gastric mucosa as the producer of pepsin and hydrochloric acid. Cells of the gastric mucosa actually secrete mucus, which forms a protective barrier for the stomach. Protection is required because nearby cells do secrete hydrochloric acid and pepsin, which would be very harmful to an unprotected stomach.

Pepsin and hydrochloric acid are two important agents involved in the digestion of food proteins. Everything that enters the body through the mouth—starches, proteins, fats, Lauren—must first be broken down into simple chemical building blocks. Eventually, these rudimentary chemicals travel through the bloodstream and are taken up by cells for use as raw materials or fuel. The stomach remains busy for about one and a half days digesting the pizza that was wolfed down in five minutes the night before. Over the course of a year, half a ton of food must be methodically reduced by the stomach to simple chemicals.

Pepsin, the enzyme Scully cites as present in Lauren's dissolved tissue, is a type of enzyme called a protease. Proteases have recently achieved fame as targets of the latest drugs to combat HIV, the virus that causes AIDS. The job of a protease is to break the chemical bonds between amino acids in proteins. Imagine that a protein with its chain of amino acids linked one after another is like a string of different-colored beads. The number of beads on the string, like the number of amino acids in a protein, can vary from a few to hundreds. Let's say that special scissors can cut the beaded string only when a blue or red bead is to the left of a green or yellow bead. Another scissors can cut only when a white bead is to the left of a red or black bead. The two scissors are analogous to two different proteases. A protease can cleave within a protein only when it recognizes particular amino acids in a specific order.

The protease associated with HIV precisely clips a large virus protein into several smaller proteins, and only these smaller proteins can function in virus reproduction. The new drugs in the battle to conquer HIV, the protease inhibitors, stick to the viral protease and keep it from working. If the protease is disabled, the smaller viral proteins are never generated and the virus cannot reproduce itself. Pepsin, the protease made by your stomach cells, is quite different from the HIV protease, which chops only one specific protein. Pepsin needs to cut into little pieces the huge assortment of proteins that enter the mouth on a daily basis. Pepsin accomplishes its mission because it can snip between many different pairs of amino acids.

At first glance, it might seem intuitive that the stomach needs hydrochloric acid to help "dissolve" food. This is not, however, the main reason for stomach cells to make acid. Acid strong enough to digest proteins—strong enough to break the chemical bond between amino acids—would have your innards looking like the late Lauren's in no time. One reason to produce stomach acid is because pepsin can't work without it. Pepsin is initially made inside stomach cells in a form that is immature and no danger to any protein. This nonfunctional state keeps pepsin from immediately chopping into little bits the proteins in the cell that made it, which would promptly kill off such a stupid cell. To keep this from happening, pepsin becomes functional only after it encounters hydrochloric acid in the stomach, which happens only after pepsin has traveled outside the cells where it is made. Freed from the confines of cells, pepsin can concentrate on mincing ingested proteins.

Mulder is naturally curious as to why anyone would want to liquefy Lauren with digestive juices. He asks Scully if the melted woman is missing anything in particular that she possessed when alive. Scully replies that all of Lauren is present with one glaring exception. Lauren, who was listed at 165 pounds, now weighed in at a svelte 122 pounds. This sudden weight loss was achieved by the nearly complete elimination of all adipose—the tissue that contains fat—from her body. Furthermore, Scully tells Mulder that Lauren is also missing all of her oils (liquid fats) and fatty acids (the type of fats found in membranes).

While the elimination of all fat from the body seems like a worthwhile goal to many, chances of surviving in that condition would be about as likely as reanimating Lauren. Fats and oils are essential members of a class of molecules called lipids. Without fats, cells would have no membranes to surround them; there would be no insulating sheaths around nerve cells; there would be no steroid hormones like estrogen and testosterone. Even the dreaded cholesterol, made by animal cells from fats, is a required component of membranes and life. As important as fats and oils are to the body, it is a mystery to Mulder and Scully why anyone would want to melt someone for their body fat. People normally eat foods containing fats—usually more than they need—and can also make additional fats in their cells. What could anyone want with forty-three pounds of liquid human fat?

Mulder and Scully learn more about the killer by examining another victim, a previously overweight prostitute, now just melted skin and bones. The struggling woman had scratched skin off the killer's arm, which Mulder sends to the lab for analysis. While the DNA results do not reveal a match in the FBI database, the skin sample is nonetheless very informative. Mulder and Scully are astonished to discover that the killer's skin sample contains no oils or fatty acids. Mulder theorizes that the killer requires fats to survive since he doesn't make any himself. As Scully puts it, the killer is a vampire who sucks fat instead of blood.

Mulder believes that the killer secretes a digestive substance into the victim's mouth that dissolves fats but leaves other body constituents alone. Given the abundance of different fats in the body and their widespread uses in cells and tissues, it is interesting to speculate on what that digestive substance might be. Most cellular material, such as proteins, sugars, and nucleotides, dissolve in water and not organic solvents like chloroform. Pure fats and oils can dissolve in chloroform but not water. There is a problem, though. When dealing with fats in living tissue, chloroform alone will not dissolve them all. Many fats, like the fatty acids that make up membranes, are attached to other substances that don't dissolve well in chloroform. So what is a fat-sucking vampire to do? Possibly use a mixture of three parts chloroform to one part methanol, a common recipe used by scientists who need to separate fats from other tissue ingredients (you can imagine the looks I received from colleagues when I explained why I needed this information). A fat-sucking killer could spew acid and pepsin into the victim to help break up internal tissue, followed by a chaser of chloroform and methanol to separate the fats. Then it's sucking time.

Mulder asks Scully if this habit of predigesting food is a common theme in nature. Scully gives Mulder an excellent example: scorpions. Scorpions are real-life miniature monsters, eating insects and spiders and drinking their blood. Scorpions can be rather bad-tempered since their food source is so rare that they are often compelled to wait months, or even up to a year, between meals. They grab their prey with large pincers and tear it apart with their mouths. Then, just like the killer in "2Shy," scorpions spew enzymes and other salivary substances onto the prey, softening it prior to dining. If the prey doesn't happily submit to being torn apart and predigested, the scorpion can paralyze or kill it with a sting from its lethal tail.

There is a second example from nature that Scully could have given Mulder, that of the sea star, also known as a starfish. Anyone who has walked along a tide pool at low tide is well acquainted with these colorful, multiarmed creatures. Knowing how they snack on barnacles and clams may make you look twice at a starfish in the future. Starfish eat by extruding their stomachs through their mouths. The inside-out stomach is pressed against food and enzymes are secreted to tenderize the repast. The stomach and food are then swallowed and digestion continues. It is doubtful that "2Shy" could have passed muster with the television censors if the fat-eating killer had table manners closer to starfish than scorpions.

Since it is unlikely that Lauren would have gotten into a car with a giant scorpion or starfish, even on the sort of blind date that one has arranged via e-mail, Mulder proposes that the killer represents a genetically different creature derived from humans. In other words, a human mutant. Someone who is unable to manufacture his own fats, but has to rely on others for his needs. Since the major form of fat in the body are fatty acids, a mutation in the biochemical pathway that makes fatty acids from simpler chemicals would cause an individual to be unable to produce most fats. Most fatty acids are built in cells by a single metabolic pathway that requires seven different enzymes. The product of the pathway is the fatty acid called palmitate. Other fatty acids are derived from palmitate by the action of additional enzymes. If the killer had a mutation in both versions of a gene for any of the seven enzymes required to make palmitate, he would have few fats in his body and would need to ingest fats from others.

With that said, I wouldn't spend time worrying about that next kiss. Anyone who couldn't make their own fatty acids wouldn't develop from the initially fertilized egg. The first division of the first cell requires the production of membranes of which fatty acids are the major component. While Mom provides some fatty acids during development of the fetus, a whole battery of mutations would be needed for her to provide all the fats necessary for proper growth. Another slew of mutations would be required once the baby is born to produce and sequester the chloroform and methanol necessary to acquire fats from others. The need for so many mutations in so many genes to generate so many new functions will thankfully confine such mutant monsters to the safety of your television screen.

Mulder and Scully finally catch up with the killer, who is revealed to be Victor, a translator of ancient Italian with a flair for making lonely women feel needed. Victor admits to killing forty-seven additional women but is completely unrepentant. He tells the agents that while in their eyes he is a monster, he was just eating to survive. In a sense Victor felt like Typhoid Mary. The poor woman was just making a living; it wasn't her fault if people died from her cooking. Although Victor would likely get the death penalty for mass murder, even with prison cuisine he probably wouldn't last long enough to order his final meal.

How to Get a Head Without Even Trying

INT. PATHOLOGY LAB—DAY

> SCULLY
>
> Case number 2268-97, Leonard Betts. As the remains are incom-
> plete, all observations refer to a decapitated head, weight
> 11 pounds, 2 ounces.

Scully makes a visual examination of the head, feeling it with her gloved fingers—we stay on her face for this. She frowns.

> SCULLY
>
> The remains show no signs of rigor mortis or fixed lividity. Nor
> do the corneas appear clouded. This would seem inconsistent
> with the witnessed time of death, now nineteen hours ago...

Scully isn't sure what to make of this. She reaches for:
A SCALPEL
Which flashes in the light as her gloved fingertips pick it up.

> SCULLY (O.S.)
> I'll begin with the intermastoid incision...

CLOSE ON SCULLY

As she places the tip of her scalpel behind the ear, preparing to draw it over
the top of the scalp. Suddenly—

—Betts' EYES OPEN. Startled, Scully drops her scalpel—it hits the floor with
a CLING!

> —"Leonard Betts"

Leonard Betts, in the episode named for him, is a quiet, unas-
suming man who works as an emergency medical technician and has
a knack for diagnosing cancers. While on an emergency run, his ambulance crashes violently into a truck and Leonard's head is severed

from his body. While decapitation would pose a problem for most people, it is only a temporary inconvenience for Leonard, who soon disappears from the local morgue. As usual, Scully's view on the missing body—modern-day body snatchers—is slightly more plausible than Mulder's explanation: Leonard Betts's headless corpse kicked its way out of the morgue freezer cabinet and walked out by itself. When Scully examines Leonard's head, which was left behind, she is astonished to see it open its mouth and blink its eyes. Scully wonders if this frightening incident was caused by residual chemical activity stored in cells, or was there something very strange about the deceased Mr. Betts?

Scully and a pathologist find clues to just how strange Mr. Betts is when examining a slice through the frontal lobe of Leonard's brain: there is evidence of an enormous glioma. Gliomas are tumors of glial cells, which make up the supporting tissue of the brain. Since over half of all brain tumors are gliomas, simply finding one in Leonard's brain is not unusual. What mystifies Scully and the pathologist is that every cell in the brain tissue segment appears cancerous. The brain material probably looked highly abnormal to them since cancer cells no longer participate with neighboring cells to create nice, ordered tissues. Scully and the pathologist may also have seen cells with abnormally large nuclei (the nucleus contains the cell's DNA genome), due to an increased amount of DNA that is present in many cancer cells. Some of the cells were also probably in the process of dividing when the head was severed and thus had highly condensed and visible chromosomes. Such condensed chromosomes would never be seen in normal brain cells, since normal brain cells never divide. Cancer cells, on the other hand, divide frequently. If Scully and the pathologists see abnormalities throughout Leonard's brain, they would conclude that his brain was a mass of cancer cells.

While Scully is examining Leonard's head, Mulder pays a visit to Leonard's apartment, where he finds evidence of recent use. A mysterious black liquid is in the bathtub, which Mulder identifies from an empty bottle as providone iodine. Scully thinks that Mulder has finally lost his senses when he tells her that Leonard minus his head has been making himself at home. If Mulder had reached into the bathtub, he could have been more explicit in his explanation to Scully. Leonard was in the tub regenerating his missing head.

Mulder hypothesizes that Leonard Betts's cancerous condition might explain his regenerative powers. He suggests that cancer cells might be part of Leonard's normal state, which allows him to regenerate limbs, or even his entire body. Mulder backs up his contention by noting that providone iodine is often used by scientists to help amphibians regenerate. Scully scoffs at his explanation, saying that while salamanders can regenerate missing body parts, this is beyond the ability of any mammal. While Scully is accurately relating what was known at the time the episode was written, she probably wouldn't make such a sweeping statement today.

Since the mid-eighteenth century, scientists have been studying how amphibians such as newts and salamanders regenerate sliced-off tails, limbs, jaws, and even eye tissues. Less noticeable but equally important to the amphibians is the ability to regenerate heart muscles and spinal cords. The process that amphibians use to accomplish such feats of self-repair is becoming clear as scientists compare regeneration of missing limbs with the natural generation of the same limbs in an embryo. In the early stages of development from a fertilized egg, an organism's cells are immature; their fates can still be changed. This was discovered from experiments on frog embryos. When a frog embryo is only a few hundred cells old, a piece of tissue destined to become skin can be cut away and transplanted to the "brain" region of another embryo. The grafted tissue eventually becomes part of the brain. If a piece of future skin is removed from an older frog embryo, it still becomes skin even if transplanted into the "brain" region. The fate of the cells were already determined. For most organisms, the route toward cell specialization is a one way-street, with cells maintaining their specialized identities until they die.

Amphibian cells have learned the secret of turning back the clock, of losing their specialization and reverting back to a time when any fate was possible. When a newt or salamander loses a leg, the wound is healed and the process of growing back the limb begins. In a manner that is still poorly understood, bone, skin, and blood cells at the site of the wound regress back to a time when they had no identity. This newly generated mass of virgin unspecialized cells, called a blastema, then starts rapid cell division. Chemical signals are received by the growing mass of blastemal cells, causing them to learn new roles and form the missing limb.

Outside of Mr. Betts, only two types of human cells are known to regenerate—blood cells and liver cells. This regeneration is different from what occurs with amphibians. When a mammalian embryo is developing, a few cells are set aside before they become specialized. These cells, called stem cells, are able to replenish blood lost to wounds or liver cells that die during the normal course of life. Bone marrow also contains stem cells that, at least in plastic dishes, can become all sorts of different cell types—muscle, fat, bone, or cartilage—depending on what nutrients they are given. Very recently, Italian scientists found that if they injected bone marrow cells into the bloodstream of mice with damaged muscles, the cells traveled to the site of the damage and became new muscle cells. What is true for mice, though, may not be true for humans. It is well known that adult human muscle cells once destroyed are not replaced. Stem cells have also been found in the mammalian central nervous system. These cells, when combined with various nutrients, can change into any of the three major cell types of the adult brain, at least in the laboratory. What role the stem cells of the central nervous system play inside a mammal isn't known.

So what are the chances that regeneration of human body parts will leave the world of science fiction and enter the world of science? Not as remote today as they were when Scully told Mulder that mammals can't regenerate. This leap in our understanding of what the future may hold comes from a completely unexpected observation by a scientist who was studying the immune system. Ellen Heber-Katz of the Wistar Institute in Philadelphia made a routine request of her technician: poke holes in the ears of laboratory mice so that they can be tagged for identification at a later date. When Dr. Heber-Katz was ready to insert the tags a few weeks later, not a glimmer of the holes could be found. The wounds were not merely healed, it was as if the holes had never existed in the first place. Thinking like Scully, Dr. Heber-Katz made the logical assumption that the technician had simply forgotten to make the holes. A few weeks after new holes were made, they had again disappeared without a trace.

These strange happenings opened the mind of Dr. Heber-Katz to a remote but tantalizing possibility: What if the mice had regenerated the tissue and cartilage to fill in the holes? Looking closely at the process of how the mice ear tissue filled in the gaps, she noticed the presence of blastema, the same masses of unspecialized cells found in amphibians that are re-forming limbs. The mice seemed to be undergoing genuine regeneration, even though mice, like humans and other mammals, shouldn't have this capability. Dr. Heber-Katz next tested if any other parts of a mouse could regenerate. Clipping off a half inch of tail led to an amazing 75 percent regeneration.

You are probably expecting me to tell you what happened when she chopped off a leg. The reason why I don't have this information is somewhat obvious: without cauterization, which would invalidate the experiment, the mouse would die from massive blood loss before there was even a remote possibility of regeneration. So unfortunately, the full extent of the regeneration abilities of these mice is not known.

A disclaimer is probably needed at this point: DO NOT ATTEMPT THESE EXPERIMENTS ON YOUR PET MOUSE! While Dr. Heber-Katz's unusual healer mice are not visitors from the void, they are also not ordinary mice. The mice that regenerate had damaged immune systems and were being used to study diseases that involve the immune system, like multiple sclerosis. Amphibians that regenerate also have virtually no immune systems. A key experiment was performed on the healer mice that pointed to their malfunctioning immune systems as the reason why they were able to regenerate. Adult healer mice, which no longer regenerate as quickly or as well, were treated to destroy their T-cells, the immune cells from the thymus. Then the adult mice healed just fine.

Dr. Heber-Katz's speculations as to why mice have a cryptic ability to regenerate are fascinating. What if mammals like mice and humans share with amphibians the genes necessary to regenerate missing tissues but that T-cells in some way keep these genes from functioning? She believes that organisms originally had two ways of healing wounds—an immune system and regeneration. Sometime during evolution, when both systems were becoming more complex, the immune system and regeneration became incompatible with each other and a choice was necessary. While regeneration may at first glance seem like the better choice, T-cells are the body's main weapon against tumors. What would be the point of being able to replace a lost arm if the body succumbs at an early age to rampant malignant cancers? Dr. Heber-Katz believes that the very immune system that protects us from pathogens and cancers is suppressing our natural ability to engage in self-repair.

It's tantalizing to imagine a day when science can alter cells near a damaged spinal cord or amputated limb such that regeneration and a functional immune system are not at odds with each other. No one would fear amputation because the limb would simply grow back. Heart muscles damaged by disease could re-form like new, and spinal cord injuries would no longer confine victims to wheelchairs. Leonard Betts, having regenerated his head, suffers only temporary pain and inconvenience later in the episode when he tears off a thumb to free his hand from handcuffs. He knows that the thumb will grow back.

While regenerating limbs or a spinal cord may one day be science and not science fiction, regenerating a head, as Scully points out, is another issue entirely. Mulder correctly reminds her that worms can regenerate their heads. Chop a one-inch planaria worm into three hndred little pieces and in a few days, three hundred new worms are swimming around. Worm regeneration involves the same type of blastema as found in amphibians and the healer mice, but the blastema form in a different manner. Instead of cells near the wound reversing the clock and losing their identities, worms contain cells called neoblasts throughout their bodies that remain in an immature state. As long as a neoblast cell is present in a chopped worm segment, it can start dividing and generate the cells necessary to "fill in the gap," even if that gap includes the head and most of the worm. Scully is correct to remind Mulder that while worms can regenerate their heads, Leonard Betts is no worm.

So what is Leonard Betts? The possible relationship between the immune system and regeneration throws a whole new light on the mystery. Leonard's immune system must be highly compromised to allow so many cancer cells to be present, and a damaged immune system may be necessary for his regeneration abilities. It is also possible that Scully and the pathologist mistook blastema for tumors, and that Leonard's innate ability to regenerate comes from the ability of his cells to easily lose their identities, form blastema, and then gain new identities.

This possibility seems more likely than Mulder's suggestion that

Leonard is a mutant whose every cell is predisposed toward cancer. Why my theory is somewhat more plausible requires a brief digression into the nature of cancer. Cancer cells, like blastemal cells, have lost their specialized nature, but unlike blastemal cells, they are not capable of ever regaining an identity. Cells form blastema without any permanent changes to their DNA—in other words, no mutations are necessary. For a cell to become a cancer cell, mutations need to occur in many genes in that one cell. Once these genes are mutated, getting rid of the mutations and reverting back to normal isn't an option.

Healthy cells don't become cancer cells by acquiring mutations in just any genes. Cells are kept on an even keel, dividing when they are supposed to and cooperating to form tissues in the body, by two important sets of genes: proto-oncogenes (precancer genes) and tumor suppressor genes. Once mutations occur in some mixture of these genes, cells irrevocably change into cancer cells.

The function of a normal proto-oncogene is to help the cell understand when it is time to grow and divide and when it is time to rest and relax. Normal cells are highly disciplined. They divide only when they receive the proper signal that the time is right, which is relayed through a series of commands beginning with a protein on the surface of the cell's plasma membrane. The surface protein acts like a light switch. When in the normal "off" position, the cell is at rest with no thoughts of dividing. When the surface protein comes in contact with a specific substance—a growth factor—floating in the bloodstream, the protein is switched "on." Orders are then passed from this activated protein to a series of other proteins in the cytoplasm and finally to proteins in the nucleus. The nuclear proteins turn various genes on or off, which sets the cell on the path toward splitting in two. When the growth factor that started the process is no longer in the bloodstream, the surface proteins stop contacting the growth factor and revert to the "off" position. Signals cease being transmitted down the chain of proteins and the cell stops further divisions.

If any of the proteins in this chain of command decide to ignore orders from above and incessantly transmit a "go for it" signal to the remaining proteins in the chain of command, then the cell is instructed to divide and divide and keep dividing regardless of whether it is really supposed to be doing so. Through enormous strides in recent research, it is becoming clear that many of the genes for the command-chain proteins are proto-oncogenes. When a proto-oncogene is mutated, it is converted into a cancer-causing gene known as an oncogene. A defective protein is produced from the oncogene that permanently relays orders for the cell to divide. Normal cells have two undamaged versions of every proto-oncogene. It only takes one mutated version of a proto-oncogene to start a cell down the dangerous route of unchecked cell division, the hallmark of a cancer cell.

If the DNA in Leonard Betts's cancer cells was scrutinized, more than one proto-oncogene would probably be found in mutant form. Cells that become cancerous and form tumors usually have several mutated proto-oncogenes. Scientists interpret these results to mean that mutations are required in a number of different genes in a single cell to lead that cell down the path toward cancer. Cells with mutant proto-oncogenes are like cars with one foot permanently on the accelerator. Fortunately, there is still a second foot on the brakes. The brakes are applied by the protein products of tumor suppressor genes. These genes are aptly named because the proteins specified by tumor suppressor genes stop or suppress cells from dividing when they shouldn't. A disastrous situation arises when a cell that already has mutant proto-oncogenes also gets mutations in tumor suppressor genes. Without brakes, there is nothing to stop a cell with mutant proto-oncogenes from nonstop divisions, leading to a gang of identical cells that also keep dividing. Out of the trillions of cells in a person's body, it only takes one with mutations in a few proto-oncogenes and tumor suppressor genes to start a tumor that can doom all the other cells if not destroyed.

For Leonard Betts's cells to become cancer cells, both versions of at least one important tumor suppressor gene are probably mutated—most likely the gene with the unusual name of p53. p53 is named for the gene's protein product (the "p" stands for protein, and "53" stands for the weight of that protein in tiny kilodalton units[1]).

---

[1] The dalton, also known as an atomic mass unit or amu, is the basic unit of mass on the atomic scale. One dalton is defined as one-twelfth the atomic weight of carbon. A kilodalton is 1,000 daltons, and p53 therefore has the same mass as approximately 4,400 carbon atoms.

The p53 protein is so important that it is known as the guardian of the genome—the brakes in the cellular automobile. When you understand how the p53 protein performs its guardianship duties, it becomes clear why mutations in the p53 gene accelerate cells down a one-way path to disaster.

The duty of the p53 protein is to keep mutations out of a cell's DNA. It only takes a single rogue cell to become a tumor, so keeping your DNA free from mutations that just might strike important genes is clearly in your best interest. p53 can't replace the sunscreen lotion so important in shielding your cells from the sun's radiation, nor can it stop you from inhaling DNA-damaging chemicals from smoking cigarettes. What the p53 protein can do is monitor the DNA of a cell for damage due to chemicals or radiation. If p53 senses that the DNA has been harmed, it literally stops the cell in its tracks and refuses to let it divide until the cell has repaired its damaged DNA. If injury to the DNA of a cell is extensive, then p53 causes the cell to commit suicide before it can become a cancer cell and harm the body.

When the p53 guardian is absent from a cell because random mutations just happen to hit both versions of the p53 gene, the consequences are severe. No longer will that cell stop dividing long enough to repair any damaged DNA and no death awaits a severely compromised cell. Mutations begin accumulating throughout the genome of the cell because the cell doesn't stop to repair the damage. The more mutations that strike the genome, the more chances that some of them will land in proto-oncogenes or tumor suppressor genes. It's no wonder that the cancer cells in about half of all tumors have mutations in both versions of the p53 gene.

If many of Leonard Betts's cells are truly cancerous as Scully and the pathologist believe, then examination of Leonard's DNA would probably reveal that he has inherited two faulty versions of the p53 gene. Normally, this condition is fatal. Mice without at least one normal version of the p53 gene in every cell die within a few weeks of birth riddled with tumors. Based on the mice studies, only fictional people like Leonard could survive with two faulty versions of the p53 gene in every cell.

If an early death awaits an individual who inherits two bad versions of the p53 gene, what are the consequences of inheriting one faulty version of the gene? This would mean that every cell in a person's body has the distinct disadvantage of starting life with only one good version of their genome guardian. While a single version of the gene produces enough p53 protein to guard a cell, all cells are only a single mutation in the remaining good version of the p53 gene away from disaster. The odds that some cell of that person's body will be struck by a mutation in the remaining good version of the p53 gene are much higher than the odds that two independent events will knock out both p53 versions in a cell of a normal person. If you win the lottery, the odds are much greater that you will win again before your jealous neighbor wins twice. If you have just one normal version of the p53 gene in your cells, then any of the 100 trillion cells in your body need only a single mutation in that remaining gene to lose its genome guardian.

In 1969, F. P. Li and Joseph Fraumeni were studying the genealogy of families that had many members afflicted with cancer at an early age. They discovered that a predisposition to cancer could be inherited. In 1990, the nature of that inheritance was made clear. Seventy percent of the families ravaged by a wide variety of cancers were passing along a faulty version of the p53 gene. Inheriting a bad version of the p53 gene means a 50 percent chance of developing cancer by age thirty and a 90 percent chance by age sixty. This particular predisposition to cancer was named Li-Fraumeni syndrome and afflicts one hundred known families. Inheriting mutations in other tumor suppressor genes is what predisposes additional people to more specific types of cancer, such as colon or breast cancer.

At the end of the episode, Leonard Betts traps Scully in an ambulance but she deftly turns the tables by killing him with a defibrillation machine. Apparently, Leonard's regeneration skills are not sufficient to repair the damage to his heart before it stops functioning. Before he dies, Leonard uses his uncanny—and unexplained—ability to detect cancer in others to tell a shocked Scully that she has cancer. And, unfortunately for Scully, it is not the type that allows regeneration of a diseased body.[2]

---

[2]Scully's cancer treatment lies ahead in Chapter 4.

Aliens 'R Us

INT. KENSINGTON BUILDING—NIGHT

STRUGHOLD

We've been forced to reassess our role in colonization by new facts of biology which have presented themselves.

GROUP ELDER
(speaking up)

The virus has mutated.

WELL-MANICURED MAN

On its own?

CIGARETTE SMOKING MAN

We don't know. So far, there's only the isolated case in Dallas.

STRUGHOLD

Its effect on the host has changed. The virus no longer just invades the brain as a controlling organism. It's developed a way to modify the host body.

WELL-MANICURED MAN

Into what?

STRUGHOLD

A new extraterrestrial biological entity.

—Fight the Future (the X-Files movie)

As those who have seen the *X-Files* movie already know, two Neanderthal explorers had an alien encounter in snow-covered Texas about 37,000 years ago. Since Neanderthals mainly confined themselves to Europe and western Asia, these hominids must have been the Christopher Columbuses of their generation. While exploring a large cave, they find a dead comrade frozen in the icy walls. The corpse's killer soon makes an appearance, attacking one of the unsuspecting Neanderthals with feral glee. The Neanderthal, no easy victim, slashes the creature with a knife before being overwhelmed. His companion dispatches the weakened creature, which leaks a black, oily substance onto the floor of the cave. The remaining Neanderthal has only seconds to savor his victory before being invaded by the black slime.

The underground cave is rediscovered in modern times when a Texas boy accidentally falls through a hole in the roof. Both the kid and his firemen rescuers are overcome by the black slime, still kicking after all these years. The effect of the ancient black slime on humans is not a pretty sight. It causes a lizardlike entity to develop inside the body, the same Neandercidal creature from prehistory. When the entity finishes developing, it bursts through the chest of the victim into the outside world, and indiscriminately attacks anyone nearby.

Chris Carter, the movie's scriptwriter, originally wanted to connect the black oily slime and the lizardlike entity in the following way: the black slime carries a virus, which is infectious when the slime enters a person; in the warmth of a person's body, the virus develops into the monstrous creature.

Very imaginative, yes. Minutely possible within the framework of biology, no.

After reading the movie script in early 1997, I hoped that Chris would change his mind. Having a special place in my heart for viruses, I discussed with him why a virus couldn't possibly develop into anything. Viruses are, after all, just a bag of genes. A bag of genes that turns into a lizard with large black eyes and long pointed nails wouldn't fit even my expanded definition of an extraterrestrial virus. I explored with Chris an idea for tinkering with his scenario. What if the black slime virus is responsible for the development of the creature but is not the progenitor of the creature? The virus, carried into a human by the black slime, could invade a cell in the person's body and cause the cell to lose its identity. The cell could then be enticed by the virus to enter a new developmental pathway. That cell, together with its descendant cells, would regenerate into the hideous alien monster. I was thrilled that Chris liked the changes, since I wasn't enthusiastic about the ribbing I would have taken from my fellow virologists if viruses changed into lizardlike aliens on the big screen—with me credited as science advisor.

I must confess that the idea of a foreign organism invading a living creature and redirecting the identity of some of its cells is not exactly original. A common soil bacterium named *Agrobacterium tumefaciens* sets up shop in plants after persuading the plant to build it a comfy home. The allure of the bacterium is its remarkable and unique ability to remove some of its own DNA and splice it into the genome of a plant cell. The genes on the DNA that the bacterium transfers into the plant cell cause the cell to become confused and lose its identity. The cell then begins rapid cell divisions, generating a mass of cells called a gall. While the gall doesn't continue developing into a homicidal plant monster, it does cause an unsightly lump to appear on the plant, a lump the bacteria call home. The transferred DNA also literally supplies the icing on the cake, since it causes the cells of the gall to prepare daily nutritious repasts for its tiny residents.

Knowing that *Agrobacterium tumefaciens* has the ability to redirect the identity of cells, it's not a stretch to imagine a virus that can do the same. In fact, there are a number of viruses that can insert themselves into the genomes of host cells and then pop back out. Some of these viruses carry with them mutated versions of normal cellular genes, which they stole long ago when extracting themselves out of some other cell's genome. Many of these kidnapped genes were once cellular proto-oncogenes, the precancer genes that when defective can start cells down the road to cancer. When the virus inserts itself and its stolen genes into the DNA of a cell, the stolen proto-oncogene becomes an oncogene and causes the invaded cell to begin nonstop divisions. A cell that is dividing needs to make a number of ingredients to replicate its own DNA, which are the same ingredients that the clever virus needs to duplicate itself as well.

These viruses, called tumor viruses, merely switch a cell from normal mode into cancer mode. The virus carried by the black slime has a much more demanding job. Not only does it have to cause an infected cell to become confused and lose its identity, but the virus then has to make the cell develop into something that isn't human. This would require the presence and activation of an entirely new set of genetic instructions in the human genome—instructions beyond the ones normally used to create a living, breathing, thinking person.

If the science fiction scenario of a virus activating a resident program in the genome of a human cell to cause the cell to develop into a monster is to be even remotely believable, there would have to exist in the human genome an extensive amount of DNA whose purpose is not currently known. One would think this unlikely, since after millions of years of evolution, the human genome should stand out as a shining example of the efficient use of DNA. In contrast, bacteria, being merely single-celled organisms many of which have survived virtually unchanged for over a billion years of evolutionary history, should be able to blame their inefficient genomes for their lowly status on the totem pole of life. There is just one little problem with these last two statements—the opposite is true. Bacterial genomes are highly efficient assemblies of wall-to-wall genes. In contrast, the 100,000 genes of the human genome take up less than 5 percent of the DNA in a cell. That leaves 95 percent of the human genome for . . . ?

Like all humans, your 100,000 genes turn on and off in different cells and at different times during your life. Only when genes are on and active can proteins be made from the instructions specified by the genes. For years, scientists focused on understanding the genes of an organism since it's the proteins that make us who we are. The remaining 95 percent of the human genome is known as "junk" DNA, which pretty much sums up its importance to most scientists. Although little time and money has been spent on understanding why the human genome is filled with junk, scientists have determined that much of the garbage DNA is composed of thousands or even millions of copies of tiny repeated nucleotide sequences, some as short as two nucleotides. About 1 percent of the genome is composed of remnants of past viral infections—pieces of viruses that are now trapped in the genome and can no longer pop back out. Also included in the junkyard of the genome is a small segment that is found in half a million copies scattered throughout every chromosome. These small segments, called Alu, create new versions of themselves as they hop around the genome. If an Alu segment jumps into a spot already occupied by an important gene, that gene becomes disrupted and nonfunctional. The mystery of junk DNA is this: If it's just taking up space, or is potentially harmful to important genes, why exist at all?

The very presence of junk DNA after millions of years of evolution suggests that "junk" is a misnomer. The DNA is probably there for a reason, we just don't know what that reason is . . . yet. Maybe it helps to control when genes are turned on and off, or maybe it helps to maintain the structure of chromosomes. Or maybe it's a set of instructions for the development of a lizardlike alien monster with sharp, pointed teeth.

In "The End," the *X-Files* episode that precedes the movie, a link is first presented between the human genome and the alien conspiracy that permeates many earlier episodes. A twelve-year-old boy named Gibson Praise has become a chess prodigy because he can read the minds of his opponents. Mulder is told by a man who was sent to kill Gibson that the kid is the missing link in Mulder's quest for the truth behind the paranormal events in the X-Files.

Mulder comes to believe that Gibson is the key to all spiritual and paranormal phenomena. He bases this belief on intriguing research done by Scully. She claims that neurological exams of the boy's brain reveal something peculiar in the part of the brain she calls "the God module"—a portion of the brain that may hold the secret to highly emotional religious experiences.

All manners of behaviors are now being attributed to genes. If you are shy or extroverted, intuitive or pessimistic, thrill-seeking or aggressive, chances are that you can blame your genes more than your environment. Only a few decades ago, psychologists were convinced that the environment was the main shaper of our personalities. What changed their minds were studies of twins, many of whom had been separated soon after birth. The personalities of thousands of identical twins, with their identical genomes, were compared with the personalities of fraternal twins in a famous study by the Minnesota Center for Twin and Adoption Research. Their findings? Genes determined personalities more than the environment. In a complete turnaround from earlier thinking, environment is now thought to make family members more different, rather than making them more the same.

The most interesting case to arise from this study was a pair of separated identical twins named Jim. When they were reunited in

1979, both stood six feet tall and weighed 180 pounds. They walked with the same gait and had the same gestures. Each married and divorced women named Linda and then married women named Betty. Chevrolets were their cars, and Miller Lite was their beer. They were addicted to Salem cigarettes, bit their nails, loved stock car racing, and hated baseball. These astonishing coincidences could make someone wonder which gene in the human genome makes a person like women named Betty.

Now there is evidence that religious and paranormal experiences may also be a function of genes. A group of scientists led by Vilaynur Ramachandran at the University of California at San Diego is tiptoeing around the idea that people have vivid religious experiences because of the neural machinery in the temporal lobe of their brains.

Ramachandran studies people with temporal lobe epilepsy, who experience intense religious ecstasy, a sense of "seeing God" and being one with the universe during seizures. Ramachandran believes that there is a region of the temporal lobe of the brain—termed "the God module"—which has neuronal connections that are dedicated to religion and a belief in God. It's this area of the brain that is stimulated in people with temporal lobe epilepsy when they hear religious words. These neuronal connections could have evolved over evolutionary time to encourage loyalty to a tribe, reinforce ties of kinship, or impose order and stability on the social structure. Ramachandran carefully points out that his findings do not deny the validity of religious experiences. He is only pointing to a section of the brain that is stimulated during these experiences. How someone interprets Ramachandran's results depends, as he puts it, on whether one believes that God created the mind, or the mind created God.

The temporal lobe where the putative "God module" resides is a fascinating area of the brain located just below the cerebrum. Sometimes when the temporal lobe is damaged by a stroke, people lose the ability to recognize faces. There is no loss of vision, no problems with language or reading, "face" simply stops being a useful concept in distinguishing one person from another. A second, very rare disorder involving the temporal lobe and face recognition is Capgras syndrome. People with this syndrome insist that parents, spouse, siblings, friends, and pets have been replaced with identical imposters. Some people suffering from this syndrome think that their loved ones are imposters only when they are looking at them, not when speaking to them on the telephone.

Scully tells Mulder that there is tremendous neuronal activity in the God module area of Gibson's brain, which allows him to read minds. This leads Mulder to point to Gibson as genetic proof that paranormal X-File cases can be explained scientifically. The proof, Mulder thinks, is hidden in Gibson's genome—in portions that are unused by normal people but active in Gibson. Unfortunately, before Scully can provide further evidence for Mulder's beliefs, Gibson is kidnapped and the X-Files go up in flames.

In "The Beginning," the opening episode of the sixth season, Mulder is convinced that there is a connection between Gibson and the virus involved in activating the development of the lizardlike creatures introduced in *Fight the Future*, the *X-Files* movie. Unfortunately, hard evidence is lacking. Gibson is gone and the creatures have vanished. Mulder's only piece of evidence is a trace amount of the virus that he believes is extraterrestrial. Mulder is crushed when Scully cannot support scientifically the alien nature of the virus. After running tests, Scully reveals that the virus, while of an unknown type, has the same four nucleotides in its DNA and the same twenty amino acids in its proteins as earthly viruses. She therefore concludes that Mulder is mistaken. The virus comes from Earth.

Mulder's search for hard evidence to back up his beliefs grows warmer when he learns that another alien creature is on the loose. A scientist in Arizona working to develop an antidote and vaccine for the virus accidentally pokes himself with an infected needle. Twelve hours later the creature is born, leaving a claw in the wall of his house and a gaping hole in the chest of the dead scientist. While this might seem like an extreme way to "give birth," it does not necessarily lend support to an alien origin of the creature and virus. A worm named *Caenorhabditis elegans* normally doesn't have much problem giving birth to baby worms. However, a mutation in the wrong worm gene, and giving birth no longer is an option. The mutant worm, not being too bright, doesn't realize the dangers of bearing young until the little nippers blow up Mom when they get too big.

Mulder searches for the entity in hopes of using it to bolster his claims of the existence of extraterrestrials and, of course, prevent it from killing any more people. The creature heads for a nuclear power plant, leaving Mulder to suggest that warmth is needed because the creature is still developing. Mulder comes tantalizingly close to the entity, which has violently attacked several others. In the reactor room of the plant, Mulder finds Gibson, who is helping his kidnappers locate the creature. Blocked by a locked door, Mulder can only stare in horror as the creature slices and dices the kidnapper and then disappears with Gibson. Soon afterward, the creature molts into a familiar-looking gray alien.

At the end of the episode, Scully makes one last attempt to convince Mulder not to ignore her science. She presents him with the DNA test results on Gibson Praise, the virus, and the claw left behind by the creature in the house of the dead scientist. The test that Scully performs is one that allows her to look for copies of the virus DNA in the genomes of Gibson and the entity. What she finds shocks her. Gibson and the creature have the virus DNA in their genomes. When Mulder asks if they are infected with the virus, Scully explains that it is much more than a simple infection. The viral DNA in their genomes is a genetic remnant—it has been in the human and creature genomes for a very long time. But there is more. The virus DNA is not only in the genomes of Gibson and the creature, it is in everyone's genome. But the virus DNA is no longer functional. Where once it could be activated, it now makes up part of a person's inactive junk DNA. Gibson, however, is the exception. In his genome, the virus DNA is active—its genes are turned on.

INT. X-FILES OFFICE—DAY

MULDER

I can't accept that. Not if it refutes what I know is true.

SCULLY

They're test results. DNA from the fingernail we found—matching exactly DNA in the virus you believe is extraterrestrial—

MULDER
(realizing)

—that's the connection—

SCULLY
(continuing)

—which also matches exactly DNA I found in Gibson Praise.

Mulder takes a moment. Because it changes everything.

MULDER

I don't understand. He's infected with the virus?

SCULLY
(dead serious)

No. It's part of his DNA. In fact, it's part of all of our DNA. It's called a genetic remnant. Inactive junk DNA. Except in Gibson it's turned on.

MULDER

If it's true, it'd mean the boy is in some part extraterrestrial.

SCULLY

It would mean we all are.

—"The Beginning"

Afterword

The life of a research scientist is filled with mysteries as complex as any that appear on *The X-Files*. We are Scullys: constantly questioning and exploring, formulating hypotheses, and dismissing them when supporting evidence isn't found. Much of the knowledge regarding organisms that share our planet comes from so-called "small science"—individual investigators at universities, colleges, and museums who along with their students are deciphering such mysteries as how life began and branched into millions of current species; how cells operate and communicate within complex organisms; how genes provide the blueprints for appearance and behavior; and how life deals with being surrounded by potential pathogens. As the complex layers of life are minutely peeled back, it is increasingly evident that every organism has secrets to share that help us better understand the human animal. There is so much left to learn.

The next few decades should prove immensely exciting. Just around the corner are replacement organs grown from a person's own cells, plants genetically engineered to produce vaccines and thrive without fertilizers and insecticides, treatment of diseases from the inside out with gene therapy, the tantalizing possibilities of nanotechnology, and, maybe, the discovery that Earth doesn't have a monopoly on life in the solar system. If we can clean up our ecological mistakes and avoid new ones, and control population levels so that diminishing resources are not overexploited, then the future need not be fought but rather welcomed with open arms.

The scientists who will achieve these advancements will come from today's children: children who will choose science over vastly more lucrative and less stressful careers. Koshi Dhingra, a graduate student at Columbia University, recently surveyed a large number of ninth-grade students for where they were exposed to science on television. The top answers were PBS documentaries, the Discovery Channel, news programs and . . . *The X-Files*. The students told her that they had selected *The X-Files* because of the realism with which Scully uses science; the accurate representations of jobs dealing with science; that science is used to disprove theories on aliens; and that science is used to make the supernatural seem more believable even though they understand that the supernatural events aren't realistic. Critics who claim *The X-Files* is harmful to the public's awareness of science would probably be amazed to learn how many students in my freshman biology class point to the favorable portrayal of science and scientists on *The X-Files* as one reason for their interest in science.

When *The X-Files* ends its highly successful run, I will be among the many fans who will have to find another way to spend Sunday evenings. But in addition, I will miss those late-night phone calls from Chris Carter inquiring how people can suddenly break out in reptilian scales, and oh, by the way, it needs to involve something they ate. Life just won't be the same.

Acknowledgments

This book could not have been possible without the help of a large number of people. My thanks to student researchers Sian Gramates, Shelley Schlief, Johanna Rodrigues, John Bohannon, Connie Villalba, David Klein, and Seth Eichenlaub at the University of Massachusetts as well as Koshi Dhingra from Columbia University for sharing the results of her study on where students learn science. I am indebted to University of Massachusetts colleagues Drs. Sue Leschine, Jim Robl, Guy Lanza, Sandy Petersen, Tom Zoeller, Derek Lovley, Anne Averill, Willie Bemis, Ed Klekowski, and Judit Pogany for stimulating conversations, reviewing various chapters, and help with reference material. Much thanks to scientists from other institutions, Drs. T. C. Onstott, Roy Gallant, Geoffrey Briggs, and George Martin for responding so positively to my requests for assistance. Keeping me from complicating simple stories with scientific jargon were my nonscientist readers Dori Pierson Carter, Sondra Simon, and Mayo Simon. And finally, special thanks to Chris Carter for producing a show of such quality; Bill Rosen, my wonderful editor at Simon and Schuster; Esmond Harmsworth, my agent at Zachary Shuster, for the book writing suggestion; the members of my laboratory for putting up with a year of so many distractions; and the National Science Foundation for supporting so much fascinating research, including my own work on viruses, and for their tremendous efforts in science education.